D0105399

PARIS

Like a
Local

PARIS
Like a Local

BY THE PEOPLE WHO CALL IT HOME

Contents

EAT

DRINK

SHOP

ARTS & CULTURE

NIGHTLIFE

OUTDOORS

meet the locals

YUKI HIGASHINAKANO

Born in Tokyo and raised in Paris's suburbs, Yuki is always finding new pockets of the city to fall in love with. A cultural coordinator by day, Yuki spends time browsing cosy bookshops, searching for the next community kitchen to volunteer at and living to eat (well, it's easy to in Paris).

BRYAN PIROLLI

Now Brooklyn-based, Bryan spent over a decade living in Paris, earning his PhD at the Sorbonne and French citizenship all in the same year. When he's back in Paris and not writing, teaching university students or running his LGBTQ+ tour company, he finds time to picnic along the canal and cruise the Haussmannian avenues atop his trusty cycle, Pierre-Auguste.

Paris

WELCOME TO THE CITY

Few people are prouder of their city than Parisians – or quicker to defend its quirks. Life here is lived intensely and fiercely, with a real sense of community in each *quartier*: long-time street sellers ply their trade rain or shine, and few days pass without the simple pleasures of a lazy coffee, or a debate with friends over good food. Calling the city home means making sacrifices – not least when it comes to apartment space – but locals are repaid tenfold in having Europe's best restaurants on their doorstep. Parisians might be famously haughty and aloof, but they've got reason to believe their *mode de vie* is the best in the world.

It's easy to see why Paris inspires so many: the city is inarguably beautiful. Yet while defined by Haussmannian façades and romantic vistas, it's not homogenous. You might fall in love with the symmetry of the Bassin de la Villette or the multicultural areas in the outer arrondissements where run-down bars still serve tiny espressos.

But no matter where you are, tradition holds strong. Picking up a still-warm baguette before dinner or ending the work day with a pavement-table *apéro* are necessities, not clichés.

There are, however, some clichés that locals roll their eyes at, and that's where this book comes in. We know what Parisians cherish the most, and we've brought together the people and places shaping the city's future. While it's impossible to wholly encapsulate Paris in these pages, you'll find a snapshot of its diversity. That means counter-cultural community projects as well as esoteric art collections, and where to find the best street markets as well as street style.

Whether you consider yourself a Parisian and want to unearth your city's secrets or you're looking for inspiration for your first trip, this book will help you to delve deeper. Don't settle for the best-known boulevards and brasseries. See Paris, but do it the local way.

Liked by the locals

"Sure, you'll get the Paris that you see in the movies. But the true magic of this city is in finding your own corner, an enchanting place that you feel is made just for you."

YUKI HIGASHINAKANO,
CULTURAL COORDINATOR

*From sultry summer parties to wintry wanders
through festive markets, each season brings with
it a new lease of cultural life in Paris.*

Paris

THROUGH THE YEAR

SPRING

THE GREAT OUTDOORS

As life unfurls after winter, pavement terraces spring back and days are spent watching the world go by with a coffee.

TRADITIONAL FESTIVALS

Marking the transition from winter to spring are city-wide celebrations. Riotous dragon parades kick off Chinese New Year while chapel concerts and long dinners define family time around Easter.

GAME, SET, MATCH

Parisians go crazy for the French Tennis Open in May. Avid fans book tickets to catch a game at the stadium, but most locals gather with pals at a sports bar to watch it live on screen.

PARIS IN BLOOM

Fresh flowers and cherry blossom start to line the banks of the Seine and the big parks in April, resulting in the first picnics of the year: a Parisian pastime.

SUMMER

FESTIVAL FUN

Parisians never need an excuse to party, and June is prime time for it. The Fête de la Musique sees musicians take to the streets, Pride offers up a carnival-like parade and a jazz festival gets everyone swaying. After-parties are custom, too.

ALFRESCO LIVING

Warmer weather sees life move outdoors. On sunny days, Parisians cool off along the banks of the Seine and the Bassin de la Villette, which transform into "beaches" for Paris-Plages. Balmy nights are spent hanging out along the canal and dancing at rooftop bars.

BASTILLE DAY
The city's fire stations throw infamous champagne-fuelled parties (aka the *bal des pompiers*) the night before Bastille Day. Those not too hungover line the Seine the next day to watch the 14 juillet fireworks or catch the Military Parade.

AUTUMN
CULTURAL TOURS
Parisians dread *la rentrée* (the return), when vacations end and schools go back in September. Keeping spirits high is the start of a new cultural season. Exhibitions and plays launch, and the Nuit Blanche in October offers up an all-night party of gallery events.

HARVEST TIME
Autumn brings with it the start of the wine harvest season, and wine-loving locals flock to dedicated events. Restaurants and bars also celebrate with tastings, special menus and the odd accordion player to entertain.

COSY DINNERS
When nights draw in, comfort food is the perfect antidote. Dinner parties are hosted and friends gather in restaurants for everyone's cheese favourite: raclette.

CHILLY NIGHTS
Parisians resist retreating inside until the end of autumn, drawing terrace season out into November, with restaurants and bars offering blankets and heaters.

WINTER
SPARKLY WONDERLAND
The City of Lights literally lights up to mark the start of the Christmas period, with extravagant shop displays and illuminated trees in pretty gardens.

MARKETS GALORE
Every Parisian has either gifted, or been gifted, a trinket from one of the city's Christmas markets. But it's about more than shopping, with funfair rides, traditional stalls and gourmet treats.

WINTER SALES
Fashionistas wait all year for January, when *Les Soldes* are in full swing and sales tempt the renewal of wardrobes.

There's an art to being a Parisian, from the dos and don'ts of café culture to negotiating the city's busiest streets. Here's a breakdown of all you need to know.

Paris
KNOW-HOW

For a directory of health and safety resources, safe spaces, and accessibility information, turn to page 190. For everything else, read on.

EAT

Sitting down for a meal is sacred in Paris. Most Parisians take a full hour for lunch, served from 12pm to 2pm, and tend to order a *formule* (set menu). If you need a quick bite, find a place to perch: locals don't eat as they walk. Dinners are also relaxed and start with an apéritif (pre-dinner drink), with food ready no earlier than 8pm. As mealtimes are cherished, it's key to book ahead; note that many places close on Sundays and Mondays.

DRINK

Drinking on an outdoor *terrasse* is a ritual in Paris, where café-bars are packed from the first espresso through to the last beers around 2am. As such, coffee to go isn't the norm; if you need a quick flat white, go to a speciality coffee shop.

Don't wait to be seated: draw up a chair at a table without cutlery and staff will come to take your order. Wine and beer are acceptable from noon, but you'll raise eyebrows if you order an apéritif such as a spritz after dinner. Often there's no menu: just ask for what you want.

SHOP

There's one rule to follow wherever you're shopping: say *bonjour* (hello) when you arrive and *bonne journée* (have a good day) when you leave. Many Parisians find the failure to follow these niceties very rude and offer haughty service in return. At flea markets, haggling is accepted (for the expensive items, that is – don't bother on a €5 trinket box). As you now know, lunch is a sacred time, and smaller businesses may close from around 1 to 3pm. Oh, and carry a tote bag to avoid a plastic bag charge.

ARTS & CULTURE

Most museums and galleries are, wonderfully, free to EU citizens under 26; otherwise, tickets cost around €10–15. There's usually an extra charge for the latest temporary exhibitions – a staple in many calendars. If you go to the theatre, dress smartly and carry at least €2 to tip the usher who shows you to your seat.

NIGHTLIFE

As dinners tend to end around 10–11pm (and later on the weekend), Parisians don't get serious about entertainment until late. Clubs and music venues get going around midnight, and many bars stay open until 2am. Nights are spent leisurely, whether socializing around a table or outdoors in summer. Despite the number of drinks you consume, it's not seen as acceptable to get inebriated. After-dark Parisian style is pretty casual, too, so there's little need to dress up.

OUTDOORS

Parisians live outside when they can. Picnicking is a pastime, but permission to sit on the grass isn't a given, so look out for signs before you settle. In summer, the banks of the Seine and the Canal Saint-Martin are packed with locals escaping the heat and relaxing with friends. Wherever you hang out, keep Paris pretty and take rubbish with you.

Keep in Mind

Here are some other tips and tidbits that will help you fit in like a local.

» **Keep cash handy** Contactless payments are making inroads, but some shops, markets and old-school bars are still cash only.

» **Tip, please** Service is technically included for meals, but most people tip waiters up to 10 per cent. Taxi drivers don't expect a tip.

» **Smoke outside** Smoking is allowed on most *terrasses*; just ask for a *cendrier* (ashtray) and don't drop butts on the floor.

» **Stay hydrated** Paris is home to hundreds of free drinking fountains (some even offer sparkling water), so bring a bottle.

GETTING AROUND

Central Paris is relatively small and divided into 20 arrondissements (districts) that radiate out in a clockwise spiral from the Seine. This river runs through the heart of the city: the north is known as the Rive Droite (Right Bank), and the south the Rive Gauche (Left Bank). City limits are defined by the ring road known as the Boulevard Périphérique, or Périph. While neighbourhoods outside this and the centre's "75" zip code are no longer considered "Paris" by locals, many are interesting to explore, from semi-suburbs like Saint-Germain-en-Laye to up-and-coming Pantin.

To make your life easier we've provided what3words addresses for each sight in this book, meaning you can quickly pinpoint exactly where you're heading with ease.

On foot

Central Paris is pretty compact, and you can walk from the likes of the Arc de Triomphe to the Bastille in an hour. Arrondissements are marked on every street sign, so it's hard to get too lost. Aside from the practicalities, though, strolling the city is simply a pleasure; the French even have a name for going on a wander – a *flânerie* – so it all figures. However, don't assume that the leisurely way of life in Paris extends to walking: Parisians are busy people, so avoid dawdling on the pavements (especially narrow ones). If you do need to check a what3words location, step to the side.

On wheels

With the exception of Montmartre, Paris is reasonably flat. Add to that many traffic-restricted backstreets and a network of bike lanes, and the city is a cyclist's dream. This is the only time we'll advise you not to do as the locals do: never ride on the pavement (yep, you'll see Parisians do it) and wear a helmet.

The 24-hour pioneering Vélib' scheme set the standard for bike-sharing projects around the world. There are myriad docking stations around the city, with one- or seven-day passes available online. The green bikes (normal) are free to ride for the first 30 minutes, increasing by €1 for every additional half-hour up to €4, while the teal versions (electric) start at €1. *www.velib-metropole.fr*

By public transport

When you need to travel from one side to the other, Paris has you covered. The Métro is pretty quick and runs until 2am at the weekend (plus, its Art Nouveau signage and beautifully designed stations are city emblems). Buses are less glamorous but often handy. You can buy a carnet of ten tickets, each valid for a single journey on any form of public transport, or pick up a Navigo Decouverte (unlimited weekly pass) at any station. If you're using a paper ticket, don't throw it away until you've finished your journey as spot inspections are common.

For longer trips, you'll take the RER, a web of underground-overground commuter lines. On all routes, watch out for pickpockets: passports and wallets are routinely snatched. If you're riding an escalator, stand only on the right – Parisians use the left for walking.

By car or taxi

Driving in Paris is not for the faint-hearted – think heavy traffic, one-way streets and scarce parking spots. Few Parisians drive unless heading out of the city; rent a car from Europcar to join them.

Official Taxis Parisiens, distinguished by their green lights, are safe and reliable but generally expensive. You can hail them on the street or head to taxi ranks at the major stations. Other taxi apps include the ubiquitous Uber, FreeNow and G7. They're worth considering for journeys late at night. *www.europcar.co.uk*

Download these

We recommend you download these apps to help you get about the city.

WHAT3WORDS
Your geocoding friend
A what3words address is a simple way to communicate any precise location on earth, using just three words. ///spent.spacing.storms, for example, is the code for the famous Louvre Pyramid. Simply download the free what3words app, type a what3words address into the search bar, and you'll know exactly where to go.

RATP
Your local transport service
All public transport in Paris and the wider Île-de-France region is run by the RATP. The official app is great for information straight from the source, including first and last departures of the day. You can also create travel itineraries to work out the most efficient way to reach your destination.

Paris is defined by arrondissements, each made up of village-like neighbourhoods with their own character. Here we take a look at some of our favourites.

Paris

NEIGHBOURHOODS

1st

Parisians might not live in this tourist epicentre (it's where you'll find the Louvre), but they do pop by, weaving around the crowds to pick up lunch from boulangeries and run errands. *{map 1}*

2nd

It's all about food here, which is fitting since the 2nd was once home to Paris's central food market. These days, the smells of spices and matcha tea tempt foodies along Rue Saint-Anne – or Little Tokyo, a street full of fab Japanese-owned restaurants. *{map 1}*

3rd

The city's aristocracy once lived in the Haut Marais, so it's pretty fancy. Medieval mansions, upscale galleries and cute cafés lie here, attracting chic locals who all drop by to be seen. *{map 2}*

4th

A Jewish quarter since the 19th century, Le Marais is one of the city's most multicultural areas. (Note: you won't find better falafel than in the 4th.) It's buzzing too, thanks to an influx of LGBTQ+ bars and shops since the 1990s. *{map 2}*

5th

Bookshops on every block, dive bars and young café crowds – not to mention a quick walk to the Sorbonne University – are enough for students to put down roots in the Latin Quarter. *{map 2}*

6th

This was the meeting place for writers in the mid-20th century, though it's more of a chichi area today. That said, the historic cafés of Saint Germain remain a heartland for creatives. *{map 1}*

7th

Forget the 3rd; the 7th is the real exclusive address. Yes, the Eiffel Tower is on the doorstep, but the 7th is also awash with upscale bistros, elegant architecture and a quaint village feel. *{map 1}*

8th

Famed for its shopping street, the Champs-Élysées, the 8th is where fashionistas scour luxury boutiques and mingle with glam locals. *{map 4}*

9th

Flagship department stores and top-notch theatres make the 9th a classy area. It's not all elegance, though. Near the Opéra district lies hipster Pigalle, where bars buzz until late. *{map 4}*

10th

Fast gentrifying but still genuinely multicultural, with a strong Indian community, the 10th is loved for its local grocery stores, indie coffee shops and the canal, where *bobos* (bohemian-bourgeois Parisians) pass days. *{map 5}*

11th

No other area can match the 11th's foodie scene (sorry, 2nd). Locals journey here to eat at Paris's best restaurants; think hip brunch spots and traditional bistros. *{map 3}*

12th

Ditching its gritty rep, the 12th is on the up – just ask the young families who settle here. Aside from its green spaces, the 12th is famed for the Marché d'Aligre – the perfect place to pick up snacks for picnics. *{map 3}*

13th

Since migrants from Laos, Cambodia, Vietnam and China settled here after the Vietnam War, it's been known as the Asian Quarter. It's still multicultural, home to a fab Chinatown (Europe's largest, but we're not bragging) and, naturally, the best Asian food joints in the city. *{map 6}*

14th

When painters and poets congregated here in the early 20th century, Montparnasse grew into a liberal epicentre. Okay, it's seen modernization since (cue tower blocks), but bohemian vibes live on at cafés and galleries. *{map 6}*

15th

Queuing for a table is rare in this sleepy district, given its lack of iconic sights. It may be quiet, but its foodie scene speaks volumes, and it's full of hidden gems. *{map 6}*

16th

Only the wealthiest Parisians can afford to live here, but everyone dreams about being able to. It's no wonder, considering the swanky 16th stretches along the Seine and brims with renowned museums. *{map 6}*

17th

Thanks to the hip Batignolles district, the 17th is shaking off its elite rep. It's a magnet for designers with its trendy bars and boutiques. *{map 4}*

18th

The 18th is often defined by arty Montmartre, but the Goutte d'Or – or Little Africa – is where it's at. A large African community have shaped this area, loved for its North African food trucks and Nigerian salons. *{map 4}*

19th

You know you're in the 19th when you can see green for days. Paris's two largest parks lie here – a city-centre escape where families picnic and old boys play *pétanque*. *{map 5}*

20th

Free spirits have long been attracted to multiethnic Belleville and Ménilmontant. While artists toil away in galleries, hipsters live it up in edgy bars. *{map 5}*

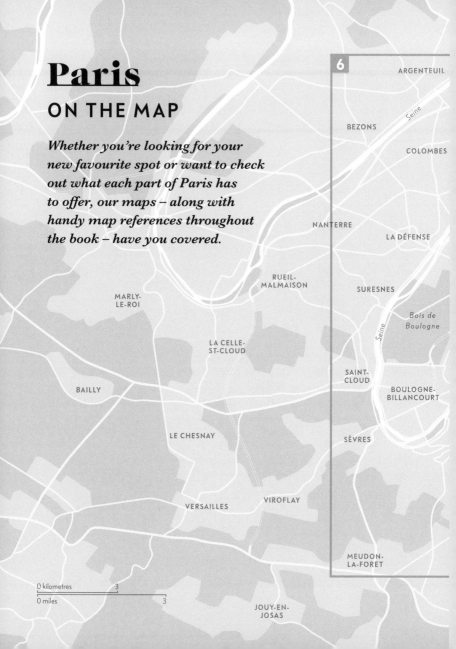

Paris
ON THE MAP

Whether you're looking for your new favourite spot or want to check out what each part of Paris has to offer, our maps – along with handy map references throughout the book – have you covered.

6

ARGENTEUIL

Seine

BEZONS

COLOMBES

NANTERRE

LA DÉFENSE

RUEIL-MALMAISON

SURESNES

MARLY-LE-ROI

Bois de Boulogne

Seine

LA CELLE-ST-CLOUD

SAINT-CLOUD

BAILLY

BOULOGNE-BILLANCOURT

LE CHESNAY

SÈVRES

VIROFLAY

VERSAILLES

MEUDON-LA-FORET

0 kilometres   3
0 miles   3

JOUY-EN-JOSAS

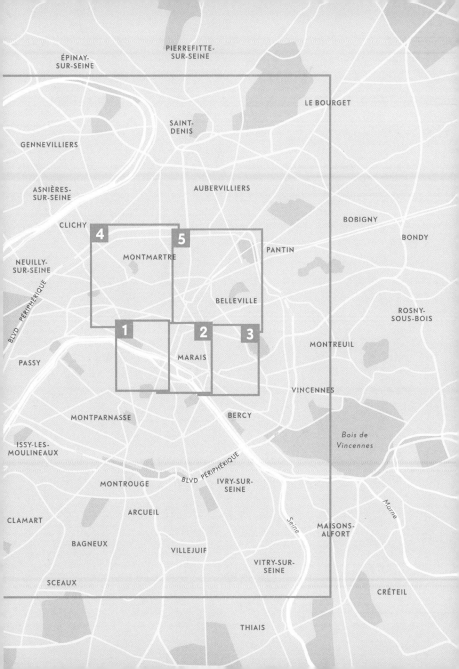

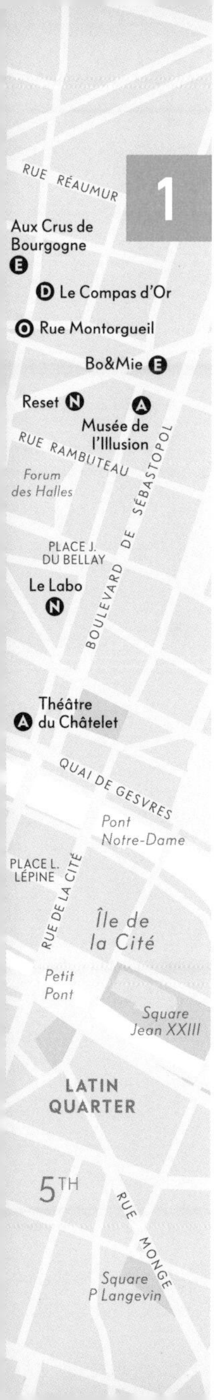

MAP 1

E EAT

Aki Boulangerie *(p33)*
Aux Crus de Bourgogne *(p41)*
Bo&Mie *(p34)*
Yasube *(p51)*

D DRINK

Le Compas d'Or *(p76)*
Freddy's *(p66)*
Treize au Jardin *(p63)*

S SHOP

E. Dehillerin *(p86)*
Kiliwatch *(p102)*
Librairie Galignani *(p96)*
Librairie Jousseaume *(p97)*
Mad Lords *(p103)*
Nose *(p106)*
L'Officine Universelle Buly *(p107)*
Oh My Cream! *(p105)*
The Red Wheelbarrow *(p99)*
Rouje *(p102)*
Shinzo *(p100)*

A ARTS & CULTURE

59 Rivoli *(p116)*
Museé de l'Illusion *(p122)*
Museé du Louvre *(p114)*
Museé du Luxembourg *(p112)*
Museé d'Orsay *(p113)*
Théâtre du Châtelet *(p127)*

N NIGHTLIFE

Le Dernier Bar avant la Fin du Monde *(p151)*
Église St Sulpice *(p147)*
Jardin du Carrousel *(p155)*
Jardin Nelson Mandela *(p155)*
Le Labo *(p156)*
Pont des Arts *(p154)*
Reset *(p149)*

O OUTDOORS

Galerie Vivienne *(p180)*
Jardin du Luxembourg *(p166)*
Jardin du Palais Royal *(p164)*
Marne River *(p175)*
Place Dauphine *(p183)*
Rue Montorgueil *(p181)*
Square du Vert-Galant *(p177)*

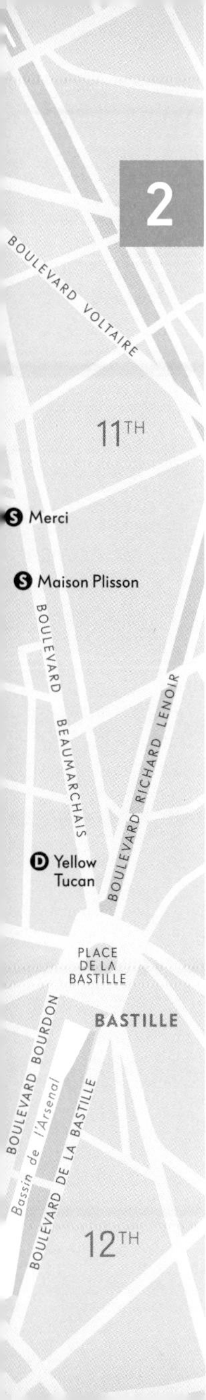
2
BOULEVARD VOLTAIRE
11TH
Merci
Maison Plisson
BOULEVARD BEAUMARCHAIS
BOULEVARD RICHARD LENOIR
Yellow Tucan
PLACE DE LA BASTILLE
BASTILLE
BOULEVARD BOURDON
Bassin de l'Arsenal
BOULEVARD DE LA BASTILLE
12TH

EAT

Au P'tit Grec *(p39)*

Baieta *(p46)*

Bar à Iode Saint Germain *(p45)*

Chez Alain (Miam Miam) *(p38)*

Elmer *(p46)*

Hank Pizza *(p53)*

Sacha Finkelsztajn *(p32)*

DRINK

La Belle Hortense *(p64)*

Bisou *(p68)*

Caféothèque *(p63)*

Comptoir des Archives *(p77)*

Les Philosophes Café *(p78)*

Le Progrès *(p76)*

Sherry Butt *(p71)*

Yellow Tucan *(p60)*

SHOP

A la Ville de Rodez *(p87)*

CSAO *(p94)*

Faguo *(p101)*

Fleux' *(p93)*

Huygens *(p105)*

Liquides Bar à Parfum *(p104)*

Maison Plisson *(p85)*

Merci *(p94)*

Papier Plus *(p96)*

Papier Tigre *(p98)*

Présence Africaine *(p97)*

Village Saint-Paul *(p90)*

ARTS & CULTURE

Black Paris Walks, le Paris Noir *(p130)*

Centre Pompidou *(p112)*

Ciné le Grand Action *(p124)*

Galerie Perrotin *(p116)*

Institut du Monde Arab *(p129)*

Maison Européenne de la Photographie *(p119)*

Musée d'Art et d'Histoire du Judaïsme *(p128)*

Musée des Arts et Métiers *(p115)*

Musée Carnavalet *(p128)*

Musée de Cluny *(p123)*

Panthéon *(p130)*

Rocky Horror at Studio Galande *(p125)*

Théâtre de la Ville de Paris *(p127)*

NIGHTLIFE

Jardin Tino-Rossi *(p154)*

Péniche Marcounet *(p141)*

Le Petit Fer á Cheval *(p158)*

Place du Marché Sainte-Catherine *(p153)*

Pont Marie *(p153)*

OUTDOORS

Place Louis Aragon *(p167)*

Place des Vosges *(p167)*

Rue des Barres *(p181)*

PLACE DE LA RÉPUBLIQUE

BOULEVARD DU TEMPLE

BOULEVARD VOLTAIRE

BOULEVARD RICHARD LENOIR

RUE JEAN-PIERRE TIMBAUD

RUE DE MÉNILMONTANT

BOULEVARD DE MÉNILMONTANT

E Café Chilango

E Pizz-art

Le Bar à Pintes

La Place Verte **E**

Chez Bouboule **N**

Musée Edith Piaf **A**

E Utopie

The Naked Shop **S**

OBERKAMPF

AVENUE DE

Le Perchoir Ménilmontant **N**

La Fine Mousse **D**

Gossima Ping Pong Bar **N**

RUE

LA

RÉPUBLIQUE

11TH

Les Mots à la Bouche **S**

D Dirty Lemon

3RD

BLVD DES FILLES DU CALVAIRE

BOULEVARD BEAUMARCHAIS

RUE DE TURENNE

D Mr Alphonse

Atelier des Lumières **A**

RUE DU CHEMIN VERT

RUE ST-MAUR

BOULEVARD RICHARD LENOIR

RUE DU CHEMIN VERT

BOULEVARD VOLTAIRE

Café du Coin **N**

E Caffé Créole

D Back in Black

Place des Vosges

PLACE LÉON BLUM

CheZaline **E**

E VG Patisserie

RUE DE LA ROQUETTE

AVENUE LEDRU-ROLLIN

BOULEVARD VOLTAIRE

RUE LÉON FROT

RUE ST-ANTOINE

4TH

BLVD HENRI IV

PLACE DE LA BASTILLE

BASTILLE

RUE DU FAUBOURG ST-ANTOINE

Waly Fay **E**

RUE DE CHARONNE

E Mokoloco

Le Chalet Savoyard **E** **E**

Les Cuves de Fauve

11TH

RUE FAIDHERBE

E Bistrot Paul Bert

BOULEVARD BOURDON

Bassin de l'Arsenal **O**

Ailleurs **S**

N Supersonic

Stroll the Coulée Verte **O**

O Cycle the Canal

Bassin de l'Arsenal

BLVD DE LA BASTILLE

Parc Rives de Seine **O**

O Jog the Parc Rives de Seine

La Seine

AVENUE LEDRU-ROLLIN

RUE DE LYON

Agrology **N**

Boulangerie **E** Bo

Confiture **S** Parisienne

N Gamelle

D Le Baron Rouge

S Marché d'Aligre

PLACE D'ALIGRE

RUE DE CHARENTON

12TH

RUE DU FAUBOURG ST-ANTOINE

RUE DE REUILLY

BOULEVARD DIDEROT

DIDEROT

BOULEVARD DIDEROT

AVENUE DAUMESNIL

MAP 3

20TH

3

AVENUE GAMBETTA

Hike through
Cimetière du
Père Lachaise

AVENUE
PHILIPPE
AUGUSTE

E Fulgurances
"l'Adresse"

BOULEVARD VOLTAIRE

RUE LÉON FROT

E EAT

Bistrot Paul Bert *(p41)*
Boulangerie Bo *(p34)*
Café Chilango *(p48)*
Caffé Créole *(p51)*
Le Chalet Savoyard *(p40)*
CheZaline *(p36)*
Fulgurances "l'Adresse" *(p45)*
Mokoloco *(p38)*
Pizz-art *(p39)*
Utopie *(p35)*
VG Patisserie *(p35)*
Waly Fay *(p49)*

D DRINK

Back in Black *(p61)*
Le Baron Rouge *(p66)*
Les Cuves de Fauve *(p72)*
Dirty Lemon *(p69)*
La Fine Mousse *(p74)*
Mr Alphonse *(p66)*
La Place Verte *(p79)*

S SHOP

Ailleurs *(p94)*
Confiture Parisienne *(p84)*
Marché d'Aligre *(p88)*
Les Mots à la Bouche *(p98)*
The Naked Shop *(p106)*

A ARTS & CULTURE

Atelier des Lumières *(p118)*
Musée Edith Piaf *(p122)*

N NIGHTLIFE

Agrology *(p156)*
Le Bar à Pintes *(p149)*
Café du Coin *(p157)*
Chez Bouboule *(p148)*
Gamelle *(p150)*
Gossima Ping Pong Bar *(p150)*
Le Perchoir Ménilmontant *(p140)*
Supersonic *(p145)*

O OUTDOORS

Bassin de l'Arsenal *(p173)*
Cycle the Canal *(p168)*
Hike through Cimetière du
  Père Lachaise *(p171)*
Jog the Parc Rives de Seine *(p170)*
Parc Rives de Seine *(p172)*
Stroll the Coulée Verte *(p169)*

0 metres   300
0 yards   300

0 metres 500
0 yards 500

BOULEVARD PÉRIPHÉRIQUE

BOULEVARD NEY

BESSIÈRES

La Recyclerie **A**

BOULEVARD

LES ÉPINETTES

A Le Hasard Ludique

RUE CHAMPIONNET

CLIGNANCOURT

RUE ORDENER

AVENUE DE SAINT-OUEN

AVENUE DE CLICHY

RUE CHAMPIONNET

Parc Clichy-
Batignolles
Martin Luther
King

Café Pimpin **D**

L'Abattoir Végétal **E**

Lamarck-
Caulaincourt **O**

N Pignon

MONTMARTRE

Square des
Batignolles

Musée de **A**
Montmartre

Cimetière de
Montmartre

17TH

Rooster **E**

PLACE
DU TERTRE

RUE DE ROME

BATIGNOLLES

RUE CAULAINCOURT

A Le Bal

The steps of the Sacré-Coeur **O**

PLACE
ABBESSES

Halle Saint- **A**
Pierre

Marché Biologique
des Batignolles **S**

BLVD DE CLICHY

Le Divan
du Monde

BOULEVARD DE

BOULEVARD DES BATIGNOLLES

PLACE
PIGALLE

AVENUE DE VILLIERS

Lulu White **D**

L'Entrée des Artistes **N**

Mamiche
E

BLVD DE COURCELLES

RUE DE CONSTANTINOPLE

RUE DE CLICHY

RUE NOTRE-DAME-DE-LORETTE

BrEAThe **E**
Restaurant

Potager de **E**
Charlotte

O Parc
Monceau

E The Grill Room

9TH

Rue des Martyrs

RUE DE LONDRES

Hanoï **D**
Corner

Mieux

D Pompette

8TH

BOULEVARD

Square de
la Trinité

E

RUE DE CHÂTEAUDUN

Musée
Jacquemart-André **A**

BOULEVARD HAUSSMANN

PLACE ST-
AUGUSTIN

RUE LA FAYETTE

MALESHERBES

Square
Louis XVI

BOULEVARD HAUSSMANN

RUE DU FAUBOURG ST-HONORÉ

Loox **S**

BLVD DES ITALIENS

PLACE
DE LA
MADELEINE

BLVD DES CAPUCINES

RUE DU QUATRE SEPTEMBRE

2ND

MAP 4

MAP 5

 EAT

Le Cadoret *(p42)*

Cantine Primeur *(p52)*

Cheval d'Or *(p47)*

Early June *(p40)*

Kiez *(p48)*

New Soul Food *(p37)*

Le Pacifique *(p49)*

Réveil du 10ème *(p42)*

Tien Hiang *(p53)*

Urfa Dürüm *(p37)*

Ⓓ DRINK

Café Chéri(e) *(p68)*

Chez Prune *(p60)*

La Commune *(p71)*

Grand Marché Stalingrad *(p79)*

Gravity Bar *(p69)*

La Marine *(p78)*

Paname Brewing Company *(p74)*

Ⓢ SHOP

BMK *(p86)*

L'Eau et les Rêves *(p99)*

Less is More *(p101)*

Marché Saint-Martin *(p89)*

Sergeant Paper *(p92)*

Taka & Vermo *(p85)*

La Trésorerie *(p93)*

Velan *(p86)*

Ⓐ ARTS & CULTURE

104 Centquatre *(p132)*

Cinéma en Plein Air *(p124)*

Le Shakirail *(p133)*

Ⓝ NIGHTLIFE

À La Folie Paris *(p150)*

La Bellevilloise *(p144)*

Canal Saint-Martin *(p152)*

La Fontaine *(p158)*

La Gare *(p146)*

Pavillon Puebla *(p143)*

Philharmonie de Paris *(p147)*

Quai de la Loire *(p152)*

Rosa Bonheur *(p140)*

Le Top du Point Ephémère *(p143)*

Ⓞ OUTDOORS

Bassin de la Villette *(p173)*

Parc de Belleville *(p178)*

Parc des Buttes-Chaumont *(p164)*

Passage Brady *(p182)*

Passerelle Richerand *(p177)*

ARGENTEUIL

SAINT-DENIS

La Seine

BEZONS

GENNEVILLIERS

COLOMBES

AUBERVILLIERS

ASNIÈRES-
SUR-SEINE

La Seine

CLICHY

BLVD PÉRIPHÉRIQUE

LA DÉFENSE

NEUILLY-
SUR-SEINE

17TH

*See maps 1–5
for Central Paris*

SURESNES

Fondation
Louis Vuitton Ⓐ

Jog the Bois de
Boulogne Ⓞ

Ⓓ La Vigne de
Suresnes

Palais
Galliera

Marché
Président-Wilson Ⓢ Ⓐ

Palais de Tokyo Ⓐ

Cité de l'Architecture Ⓐ
et du Patrimoine

Ⓐ Musée du Quai
Branly–Jacques Chirac

La Seine

PASSY

Ⓐ Pont de
Bir-Hakeim

Cravan Ⓝ

Ⓝ Musée
Rodin

16TH

Grande
Mosquée
de Paris Ⓓ

Le
Mazette
Ⓝ

Ground
Control
Ⓐ

Piscine Molitor Ⓞ

Bowling de Paris
Front de Seine Ⓝ

Niébé Ⓔ

SAINT-
CLOUD

La Javelle Ⓝ Ⓞ

Ride the Ballon
de Paris Generali

Skate with
Pari Roller Ⓝ

Vignerons
Parisiens Ⓓ

Piscine
Joséphine Baker Ⓞ

Parc de
Bercy
Ⓐ
Ⓞ

Parc de
Saint-Cloud Ⓞ

BOULOGNE-
BILLANCOURT

15TH

MONTPARNASSE

Fondation
Cartier pour l'Art
Contemporain Ⓐ

Season Square Ⓔ

Quai François
Mauriac Ⓞ

Ⓝ La Seine
Musicale

ISSY-LES-
MOULINEAUX

Find the Petite
Ceinture Ⓞ

14TH

Ⓢ

Butte-aux-
Cailles Ⓞ

13TH

SÈVRES

Marché aux Puces
de la Porte de Vanves

BLVD PÉRIPHÉRIQUE

IVRY-SUR-
SEINE

MONTROUGE

ARCUEIL

0 kilometres 2

0 miles 2

CLAMART

BAGNEUX

VILLEJUIF

SCEAUX

MAP 6

🄴 EAT

Benoît Castel *(p33)*

Niébé *(p51)*

Season Square *(p54)*

🄳 DRINK

Bar Gallia *(p75)*

Grand Mosquée de Paris *(p77)*

La Vigne de Suresnes *(p73)*

Vignerons Parisiens *(p75)*

🅂 SHOP

Marché Président-Wilson *(p88)*

Marché aux Puces de la
Porte de Vanves *(p91)*

🄰 ARTS & CULTURE

Cité de l'Architecture et du
Patrimoine *(p113)*

La Cité Fertile *(p135)*

Fondation Cartier pour l'Art
Contemporain *(p119)*

Fondation Louis Vuitton *(p118)*

Ground Control *(p135)*

Musée des Arts Forains *(p121)*

Musée Nationale de l'Histoire
de l'Immigration *(p131)*

Musée du Quai Branly–
Jacques Chirac *(p120)*

Musée Rodin *(p131)*

Palais Galliera *(p115)*

Palais de Tokyo *(p114)*

🄽 NIGHTLIFE

Bowling de Paris Front
de Seine *(p151)*

Cravan *(p158)*

La Javelle *(p143)*

Mama Shelter East *(p141)*

Le Mazette *(p145)*

La Seine Musicale *(p144)*

🄾 OUTDOORS

Bois de Vincennes *(p167)*

Butte-aux-Cailles *(p180)*

La Campagne à Paris *(p182)*

Find the Petite Ceinture *(p170)*

Jog the Bois de Boulogne *(p168)*

Parc de Bercy *(p166)*

Parc de Saint-Cloud *(p176)*

Piscine Joséphine Baker *(p175)*

Piscine Molitor *(p172)*

Pont de Bir-Hakeim *(p178)*

Quai François Mauriac *(p175)*

Ride the Ballon de Paris
Generali *(p169)*

Skate with Pari Roller *(p171)*

6

🄰 La Cité Fertile

PANTIN

🄳 Bar Gallia

🄴 Benoît Castel

🄾 La Campagne à Paris

🄽 Mama Shelter East

20ᵀᴴ

VINCENNES

Musée Nationale de l'Histoire de l'Immigration

12ᵀᴴ 🄰

🄰 Musée des Arts Forains

🄾 Bois de Vincennes

La Seine

VITRY-SUR-SEINE

EAT

Food is the soul of Paris. Good cooking and good company are held sacred in time-honoured brasseries, bistros with a modern edge and laidback dining rooms.

Perfect Patisseries

Nothing defines Paris quite like the patisserie. While it's a myth that Parisians eat croissants every morning, bread is bought freshly baked daily, and picking up a tart is more sophisticated than making your own.

SACHA FINKELSZTAJN

Map 2; 27 Rue des Rosiers, 4th; ///smirks.barmaid.debate; www.laboutiquejaune.fr

Boutique Jaune, as it's commonly known thanks to its *jaune* (yellow) façade, is the most traditional of the Yiddish bakeries in the heart of Paris's Jewish community. It's been family run for three generations and is delightfully old school: queue once to browse the breads and bagels, then again to pay with a paper ticket at the till. Shopping here has changed little since opening in 1946, only adding to its charm.

MAMICHE

Map 4; 45 Rue Condorcet, 9th; ///grading.repeated.masters; www.mamiche.fr

This neighbourhood bakery, run by a young team, is taking Paris by storm with an unpretentious approach to great baking. You won't find elaborate tarts or fussy macaron flavours, but rather pillowy orange-flower brioche, gooey brownies and perfectly baked baguettes. If you're prepared to walk the pavements with jam dripping down your chin and spend the rest of the day dusting sugar from your sleeves, pick up one of the doughnuts to go.

AKI BOULANGERIE
Map 1; 16 Rue Sainte-Anne, 1st; ///bottle.archive.orbit;
www.akiboulanger.com

Surrounded by Japanese restaurants that draw crowds at night, Aki's popularity peaks during the day. By all appearances just another Parisian bakery, it's lined with cases filled with matcha-infused favourites and classics like éclairs and mille feuilles. French pastry never really gets boring, but Aki offers a unique mash-up that you won't find anywhere else in the city – or likely the world.
» Don't leave without trying the iced matcha latte – it's not sugary like it is in Japan, so pairs well with any of the cakes.

BENOÎT CASTEL
Map 6; 150 Rue de Ménilmontant, 20th;
///familiar.quarrel.roses; www.benoitcastel.com

Any Ménilmontant local will tell you this boulangerie changed their life. Named after the pastry chef at its helm, this homely spot exudes a strong community spirit, where cheerful staff work in the open kitchen. It's at the top of one of Paris's steepest streets, so once you've made the climb, have a well-deserved signature tart – the recipes of which honour Castel's Brittany roots.

BO&MIE

Map 1; 18 Rue de Turbigo, 2nd; ///dance.broads.dunes; www.boetmie.com

Don't come here expecting a classic boulangerie experience: this creative and affordable newcomer opened in 2017 on a mission to reimagine French baking traditions. That doesn't mean compromising on quality or technique, but rather having fun with flavours. Plan to have a BFF catch-up here in the morning with a praliné *pain au chocolat,* and you'll probably still be here chatting away in the afternoon over a lemon-lime madeleine.

BOULANGERIE BO

Map 3; 85 bis Rue de Charenton, 12th;
///confined.fault.skews; 01 43 07 75 21

Imagine a watercolour painting of an archetypal French bakery – on the corner of a Haussmannian building, with picture windows and gold signage – and you've got Boulangerie Bo. The inventive patisserie creations are just as beautiful as the shop's surrounds, in the sleepy side streets near the Marché d'Aligre *(p88).* Customer

Try it!
MASTER THE MACARON

Making a signature macaron is as tricky as you might expect, but you can have fun trying with Cook'n With Class *(www. cooknwithclass.com/paris).* It runs three-hour classes so you can learn the secrets.

favourites are the gorgeous strawberry tarts with a veil of cucumber gel and delicate raspberry hibiscus meringues – but if you just came for your weekly loaf of bread you won't be disappointed.

UTOPIE

Map 3; 20 Rue Jean-Pierre Timbaud, 11th;
///heap.outlines.paving; 09 82 50 74 48

There's always a line out the door at this modern corner patisserie and boulangerie. Many bakeries specialize in either breads or sweets but, unusually, here both are equally fabulous. At busy times, the aroma of fresh croissants emerging from the ovens is tantalizing enough to have you scheming ways to jump the queue, and *pains au chocolat* disappear into paper bags quicker than the chefs can bake them.

» **Don't leave without** trying the black *charbon végétal* baguette made with activated charcoal. The latest health craze may be unusual, but it's delicious and will look great in your picnic pictures.

VG PATISSERIE

Map 3; 123 Rue Voltaire; ///visa.monopoly.wounds; www.vgpatisserie.fr

Take dairy away from French patisserie and there's not much left. Enter Bérénice Leconte, the queen of Parisian vegan pastry. Creamy mousse cake, soft croissants and seasonal crispy tartlets are made with her flawless craftsmanship and organic ingredients to fool your taste buds (and wallet – they're surprisingly affordable). It's no surprise that this eco-friendly sweet sanctuary has won the hearts of even non-vegan gourmet locals.

Lunch on the Go

Parisian lunches tend to last for either twenty minutes or two hours. While there's a time and place for a decadent lunch, most folks grab light bites to take back to the office or pause to eat by the Seine.

CHEZALINE

Map 3; 85 Rue de la Roquette, 11th; ///quench.tomorrow.january; 01 43 71 90 75

If you worship at the altar of crusty bread and salty butter, this is your place of pilgrimage. For nearly a decade, this tiny café-deli has been the go-to sandwich spot for all manner of locals. Once a horse-meat butcher (the "Z" in CheZaline replaces the "v" of *boucherie chevaline*), the shop is still delightfully retro and there's an

Try it!
MAKE A SANDWICH

The Prince de Paris ham that's generously stuffed into sandwiches at CheZaline is considered France's finest, so pick some up from A la Ville de Rodez *(p87)* to make your own treat.

old-school vibe to the proceedings, where sandwiches are wrapped in butcher paper. It's a tiny space, so tuck into your liberally buttered ham baguette as you stroll to the Bassin de l'Arsenal *(p173)*.

NEW SOUL FOOD
Map 5; 177 Quai de Valmy, 10th; ///eagles.combines.porch;
www.newsoulfood.fr

This restaurant and its additional roving food truck are spreading street-food-style dining across Paris – an exciting concept in a city where sit-down meals are sacred. Mixing culinary influences from across Africa and the Caribbean, New Soul Food is big on flavour and low on formality. You'll have to check its social pages to find the food-truck schedule, and the menu changes by day, but this is all part of the fun and why it's quickly built a large fanbase.

URFA DÜRÜM
Map 5; 58 Rue du Faubourg Saint-Denis, 10th; ///kite.bronzes.gosh

Any sandwich-loving Parisian will tell you this hole-in-the-wall Kurdish joint – set amid the chaos of discount clothing stores, bijou coffee shops and traditional butchers – is a must-visit. Despite lacking an online presence, Urfa Dürüm has a cult following thanks to the office workers who pop by for the amazing flatbreads (made as you watch) and persuade their colleagues to join them the next day. Taking in the hubbub of the adjoining street is all part of the joy of waiting.

» Don't leave without trying the incredible lamb-filled *dürüm*, the meat smoky from the grill and wrapped tightly with fresh salad.

MOKOLOCO

Map 3; 74 Rue de Charonne, 11th; ///timidly.hosts.grants

You'd be hard-pressed to find anyone who lives in the 11th that hasn't fallen in love with Mokoloco's unique flavours. This isn't your average sandwich spot: as at nearby sibling café Mokonuts, owners Moko Hirayama and Omar Koreitem have created a fun, fresh and one-of-a-kind menu that blends Middle Eastern, American and Japanese flavours and ingredients. The owners still haven't created a website (or sorted a landline), but thanks to a large and obsessed fanbase, the word has spread rapidly. You'll consequently need to wait in line at lunch, when it's busiest, but the reward for missing half your lunch break are unreal katsu brioche buns and sloppy joes. It's a real *coup de coeur* (something special), as the French say.

» Don't leave without trying Moko's famous chocolate and oatmeal cookies. They're baked to order and come warm, soft and chewy.

CHEZ ALAIN (MIAM MIAM)

Map 2; Marché des Enfants Rouges, 3rd;
///fuss.exams.spot; 09 86 17 28 00

It's easy to see why the inimitable Alain has one of the longest-running stalls in the Marché des Enfants Rouges, the oldest market in Paris. First: his distinctive take on the humble sandwich. Second: his charisma – a song or dance while he whips up your lunch is pretty commonplace. As you amble through the market, you'll know you've found the right stall when you spot Alain on the *biligs* (the round cast-iron stovetops on which crêpes are sizzled), preparing food for the longest queues. Tourists come for the enormous buckwheat

If you'd prefer to tackle hot pancakes with a knife and fork, head to Alain's nearby sit-down spot at 26 Rue Charlot.

galettes, but those in the know order his sandwiches and *socca* (chickpea pancakes). All are impractical to eat, but that's just part of the fun. *Miam miam!*

AU P'TIT GREC

Map 2; 68 Rue Mouffetard, 5th; ///respect.jeep.star; www.auptitgrec.com

Among the kitschy English menus of Rue Mouffetard, this place remains a local favourite, not least among students. If there's no line, count your blessings. The crêpes here are hearty and slightly sinful but far from elegant, with creative concoctions like l'Italien, with coppa and mozzarella, proving a big hit. This spot is the only worthwhile choice for a picnic in the nearby Arènes de Lutèce, but you'll want to have a few extra napkins on hand.

PIZZ-ART

Map 3; 41 Rue Jean-Pierre Timbaud, 11th; ///appear.dramatic.tags;
www.pizzartparis.fr

Pizza by the slice might sound like just the ticket amid rue Jean-Pierre Timbaud's student bar scene, but this is no late-night dive. In fact, it closes long before said bars empty out. Swing by for lunch, the busiest time for those craving the top-quality ingredients – creamy *mozzarella di bufala*, taleggio, San Marzano tomatoes – that set the Roman-style pizza a world apart from other imitators. If you don't have a nearby office or apartment to take your slice back to, eat perched outside if it's sunny, perhaps even with a glass of wine.

Cosy Dinners

A late, lazy dinner is the Parisian way. Make a reservation for 8pm at the absolute earliest, settle in for two courses and dessert, and let the awaited catch-ups commence between it all.

EARLY JUNE

Map 5; 19 Rue Jean Poulmarch, 10th;
///shopper.dare.blaring; www.early-june.fr

Eating at this cool bar-restaurant is like dining at a friend's home, where dishes are made one by one in the tiny kitchen and delivered to every table that orders at the same time. Reserve a candlelit table and settle in for the evening to swap news over sharing plates and orange wines. Set back from the canalside melee, Early June is missed by those who venture no further than the *quais*, so it's a nicely kept secret.

LE CHALET SAVOYARD

Map 3; 58 Rue de Charonne, 11th;
///bills.vine.juggle; www.chalet-savoyard.fr

Meals centred around melted cheese are Parisian essentials during the winter. If you've not yet purchased your own raclette machine, this is where to come for a true taste of the Alps, where tables are

Make like the French and throw your own raclette party. Head to Fromagerie Beaufils in the 20th to pick up the cheeses in season. laden with pots of fondue that get gloopier by the minute, and enormous wheels of Morbier sizzle under table-top grills. It's a sociable feast, where cheese comas and good conversations linger.

AUX CRUS DE BOURGOGNE

Map 1; 3 Rue Bachaumont, 2nd; ///foods.goggle.presses;
www.auxcrusdebourgogne.com

Get ready to feast on bold Burgundian specialities: that means *escargot* that will leave garlic butter dripping down your chin and *steak-frites* smothered in Béarnaise. The wood-panelled dining room couldn't look more old-fashioned, but it attracts a cooler crowd of intellectuals and creatives lured by the novelty of countryside fine dining in the heart of the city. There's nowhere better to discover the authentic cuisine of Burgundy, France's hallowed wine region.

BISTROT PAUL BERT

Map 3; 18 Rue Paul Bert, 11th; ///dragons.held.suitcase; 01 43 72 24 01

Truly deserving of its many accolades, this is the perfect French bistro. From the tiled floors to the polished tables, it's all about tradition here. Owner Bertrand Auboyneau is a bit of a legend among the city's gourmands, but there's no pretention: expect a warm welcome and plenty of help deciphering the chalkboard menus.

>> Don't leave without trying the Grand Marnier soufflé. This oh-so-fluffy, liqueur-spiked masterpiece is as decadent as they come.

RÉVEIL DU 10ÈME

Map 5; 35 Rue du Château d'Eau, 10th;
///recent.swanky.napped; 01 42 41 77 59

Shaking off any notion that traditional bistros are unwelcoming and stuffy, this casual spot thrives on its exceptionally friendly staff and hearty portions, long making it a much-loved meeting place for all manner of crowds. Inside you can expect an older clientele playing the odd game of cards amid generous wine pourings and families tucking into enormous salads at red-check tablecloths. It's the cute terrace tables beneath the scarlet awnings that are the most coveted seats, though, so arrive early to be in with any chance of getting a good people-watching spot as the sun goes down.

LE CADORET

Map 5; 1 Rue Pradier, 19th; ///hounded.posed.smoothly; 01 53 21 92 13

With mosaic floors and mirror-backed banquettes, Le Cadoret may look traditional, but it's a subtle reinvention of a neighbourhood bistro for Belleville's increasingly "bobo" (bourgeois-bohemian) residents. Even before service starts, folks stop off to pinch one of the pavement tables or peruse the menu with a drink as they lean on the bar. The wine list is the restaurant's crowning glory: a who's who of pioneering natural winemakers that draws devotees from across Paris (much to the dismay of Belleville locals, who would rather keep this place a secret). Get chatting to the staff for the best bottle recommendations.

» **Don't leave without** trying the *tête de veau*, which, surprisingly, has never been so on trend. Boiled calf's head doesn't sound delicious, but this rich, gelatinous dish is done so well here.

Liked by the locals

"In the bistro, there are rules. Rosé is for an apéritif not dinner, the chef's word is final and don't even think about changing cutlery between courses. But this – and the cracked tile floors, the burnt robusta and the pots of wine – make me happy."

JESS TIMMINS, PARIS MANAGER AT DEVOUR TOURS

Top Formules

*The great French tradition of the multi-course meal endures. Parisians flock to the latest "it" spots for affordable mid-week **formules** at lunch, while tasting menus are reserved for celebrations at the weekends.*

MIEUX

Map 4; 21 Rue Saint-Lazare, 9th; ///asteroid.star.tricks; www.mieux-restaurant.com

Run by friends, for friends, this trendy spot is one of the city's new guard of neo-bistros. The two-floor dining room gives off the vibe of an effortlessly cool apartment, particularly when candlelit without

Hidden inside Napoleon's imposing Église de la Madeleine is Le Foyer de la Madeleine (*www.foyerdelamadeleine.fr*), a galleried, not-for-profit lunchtime-only restaurant that's become a well-kept secret among office workers and students in the area. Expect to spend around €20 on a tasty three-course lunch including cheese and dessert, or half that if you purchase an annual membership. It's a steal.

even a hint of a cliché at night. With a low-cost, three-course lunch *formule* (led by what produce is in that week), it's little wonder Mieux is popular with the start-up crowd who work in the "Silicon IX" nearby.

FULGURANCES "L'ADRESSE"

Map 3; 10 Rue Alexandre Dumas, 11th; ///finishes.struggle.student;
wwww.fulgurances.com

You never know what will grace the menu at this one-of-a-kind spot, where rising stars are invited for residencies to hone their menus before branching out solo. This means exceptional-quality cooking for a fraction of what you'd pay in a Michelin-star dining room – and bragging rights that you've discovered the next big culinary trends. Plan to spend around €40 on a multi-course meal at lunch or closer to €80 with wine at a treat-the-parents dinner.

BAR À IODE SAINT GERMAIN

Map 2; 34 Boulevard Saint-Germain, 5th;
///cone.original.mere; www.baraiode.fr

The no-frills approach to serving seafood straight from the Brittany and Normandy coasts is a breath of fresh (and salty) air here. This casual spot is a short stroll from the busiest part of the Boulevard, so you're unlikely to stumble upon it without a recommendation. Die-hard fans will tell you to head here at lunch for the bargain set menu, which is always seasonal and always delicious.

» Don't leave without trying a glass of Muscadet: the classic pairing with shellfish. If you find a bottle you like, you can buy it to take away.

ELMER

Map 2; 30 Rue Notre Dame de Nazareth, 3rd;
///cocktail.hung.stretch; www.elmer-restaurant.fr

Stylish "working" lunches and dinners with friends are the name of
the game at this elegant restaurant, set on a road lined with classic
white-shuttered apartments. A great-value *formule* (ranging from a
two-course set menu to a four-course midday tasting menu) is really
set apart by the warm service, so you'll feel comfortable lingering
here for hours while tucking into classic French food with a twist.

ROOSTER

Map 4; 137 Rue Cardinet, 17th; ///uproot.drove.zest;
www.rooster-restaurant.com

Frédéric Duca's Batignolles restaurant is reason alone to schlep to
the 17th. Duca hails from Marseille and southern flavours shine on
his bistronomy-style menu. You can rack up a serious bill if you choose
the full tasting menu with wine pairings (essential) at dinner, so opt
for the two-course lunch if you're not celebrating a special occasion.

BAIETA

Map 2; 5 Rue de Pontoise, 5th; ///outdone.nutrients.bring;
www.restaurant-baieta-paris.fr

In a city where the fine-dining scene remains heavily dominated by
men, a Michelin-starred restaurant from the country's youngest
female chef is something to celebrate. Julia Sedefdjian's restaurant
is as minimalist as they come, designed to amplify the flavours and

After your meal, head to Baieta's sister bar Bô around the corner. It stocks more than 70 niche rums from across the Caribbean.

beauty of her Niçoise-influenced dishes. Splash out on the four-course "initiation" menu at lunch and you're sure to fall in love – the restaurant's name means "little kiss" in the Niçois dialect, after all.

CHEVAL D'OR

Map 5; 21 Rue de la Villette, 19th; ///boat.marble.dominate; www.chevaldorparis.com

Everyone in Paris is talking about Taku Sekine's cooking. Despite the hype, this self-styled Franco-Asian restaurant remains a calm, family spot, where pushchairs get squeezed between tables and dishes are shared on handmade ceramics. While the mini menu isn't technically a *formule*, it offers a taste of Sekine's skill with a comfort food twist – think ramen or Sichuan-spiced chicken wings. Lunches are only served at the weekend, so book ahead or drop by for dinner instead.

THE GRILL ROOM

Map 4; 73 Rue de Monceau, 8th; ///supplied.delved.trendy; 01 42 89 59 26

Brunch may not be the biggest deal in Paris, but this glitzy spot is leading a hollandaise-smothered revolution. The vibe here is chic but not stuffy, so dress up to start your day with bubbles and a set four-course brunch while catching up with friends.

» Don't leave without trying the *brioche perdu* – decadent "French" toast drizzled with a salted butter caramel sauce.

Global Grub

After many decades of French cooking reigning supreme, the diversity of the Parisian dining scene is finally getting the accolades it deserves, with cuisines from Senegalese to Chinese being celebrated.

CAFÉ CHILANGO

Map 3; 82 Rue de la Folie Méricourt, 11th;
///restless.stapled.raves; www.cafechilangoparis.com

Parisians know that finding authentic tacos and quesadillas is as rare as scoring an affordable apartment with a balcony in the city. Banish visions of guacamole served with ready-salted crisps (yep, it's more common than you'd think): this Mexican-run spot is the real deal, bridging the divide between restaurant, taqueria and bar. It's the kind of place where you can add a stool to the table when another friend turns up for margaritas and good vibes.

KIEZ

Map 5; 90 Quai de la Loire, 19th; ///careless.noting.pints; www.kiez.fr

A modern German beer hall isn't what you'd expect to find on the banks of the Bassin de la Villette, yet it's a welcome discovery. Parisians are rarely rowdy, but the music can get loud here, setting the mood for the selection of big beers and even bigger dishes. A meal at Kiez is like taking a trip to Berlin via Bavaria: almost every Brauhaus classic – *currywurst*, *käsespätzle*, schnitzel – has appeared on the menu, and it's all washed down with Pilsner, *dunkel* or *helles* beer.

LE PACIFIQUE

Map 5; 35 Rue de Belleville, 19th; ///outfit.crystals.chew; 01 42 49 66 80
Taking up a corner spot within Belleville's misnomered "Chinatown" is this charming neighbourhood joint serving up Cantonese-style dim sum and roast meats. The banquet tables are as traditional as they come, seating regulars who celebrate the same few restaurants in the area without a tourist in sight. The smell of roast duck wafting through the room is sure to convince you to order just one more dish.
» Don't leave without trying the Cheung Fun, Chinese rice pancakes that are filled with roasted pork.

WALY FAY

Map 3; 6 Rue Godefroy Cavaignac, 11th;
///trample.logic.squeaks; www.walyfay.fr
This isn't the kind of spot you only come to once. The benches inside this low-key restaurant are always filled with a regular clientele who return for the delicious Senegalese and other West African dishes that they rave about to their friends. Service is warm and relaxed, if decidedly leisurely in comparison to the usual Parisian pace, so it feels like a home away from home. Come hungry: whether you order fried plantain or grilled chicken, portions are enormous.

Solo, Pair, Crowd

No matter where you are in the city, or how many people you're with, you're never far from a memorable meal.

FLYING SOLO
Sushi for one

Pull up a stool at the laid-back Rice & Fish in the 2nd for a solo sushi feast of sashimi, temaki and mochi for dessert. This is a meal you definitely won't want to share.

IN A PAIR
Embrace the kitsch

Parisians, usually fans of the understated, pack into Kodawari Yokochō in the 6th for its OTT Tokyo-themed décor and affordable ramen. Arrive with your bestie at 6:30pm for a catch-up without the fuss.

FOR A CROWD
Head for Hunan

A big group isn't a problem at L'Orient d'Or in the 9th, where lazy Susans are laden with the likes of cumin-spiced lamb and smoked beef with bird's-eye chillies for the whole party to dip into.

NIÉBÉ

Map 6; 16 Rue de la Grande Chaumière, 6th;
///selling.smug.copiers; www.restaurantniebe.com

This slick soul food restaurant is the antithesis of the fussy, dimly lit brasseries that typify Montparnasse. Named after the symbolic *cornille* (aka the black-eyed pea, which is native to Africa), Niébé doles out a fusion of Brazilian and African cuisine in an inviting, bright room. Many dishes are vegan, too.

YASUBE

Map 1; 9 Rue Sainte-Anne, 1st; ///secondly.flinch.central; 01 47 03 96 37

Standing out among the many Japanese restaurants that fill a neighbourhood dubbed "Little Tokyo" is this little gem. You can get great sashimi and tempura here, but it's the yakitori grilled in front of you that draws fans (who don't mind spending the rest of the day enveloped in the sweet scent of smoke after sitting too close to the grill).

CAFFÉ CRÉOLE

Map 3; 62 Boulevard Beaumarchais, 11th;
///supply.resides.trap; www.caffecreole.com

When laidback Antillais beach dining meets French café culture, this is the result: a classic Parisian façade and pavement tables backed by an uber-colourful bar stacked with rum. While an ocean breeze is lacking, homemade dishes will transport you across the Atlantic.

» Don't leave without trying The Diamond Rock cocktail: *rhum agricole* with triple sec and lime juice, sweetened with sugar syrup.

Veggie and Vegan

*While some old-guard chefs still present vegetarians
with chicken stock-spiked sauces and a shrug, meat-
free cooking is on the rise, led by a new generation of
plant-based foodies and forward-thinking restaurants.*

CANTINE PRIMEUR

Map 5; 4 Rue Lemon, 20th; ///revives.dreams.sugar; www.cantineprimeur.fr

You'd never guess that this lunchtime-only spot, with its conventional café-cantine façade, is a plant-based restaurant. It's a far cry from other vegan spots across central Paris, where style sometimes takes precedence over substance. Instead, the menu here speaks volumes: it's seasonal, but some dishes – the bo bun and three-veg lasagne – make regular appearances. Set on a quiet street back from traffic-choked Boulevard de Belleville, you need to know it's here to find it.

JAH JAH BY LE TRICYCLE

Map 4; 11 Rue des Petites Écuries, 10th;
///pints.rejected.amount; 01 46 27 38 03

It's rare to chat to your neighbours when you're out for a meal in Paris, but then it's also rare to find an authentic canteen-style Rasta restaurant right in the centre of the city. Jah Jah bucks the rules and sets trends instead, attracting an enormously diverse clientele from office workers to students. The food is healthy in the sense that it's plant-based, but it's all about piling as much as possible on your table, whether that's huge vegan bowls with rice, avocado and plantain or burgers accompanied with enormous salads and potatoes.

HANK PIZZA

**Map 2; 18 Rue des Gravilliers, 3rd; ///premises.tracks.yell;
www.hankrestaurant.com**

Every vegan Parisian's best friend "Hank" turns his hand to pizza here. As at nearby sister restaurant Hank Burger, everything from the cheese to the truffle sauce is plant-based. Appealing to Parisian sensibilities for stylish settings and sit-down dining, the atmosphere is more cool Italian restaurant than greasy fast-food joint. Slices are served when cut so you can mix and match different toppings.

» Don't leave without trying a slice of the Dandy, topped with creamy truffle sauce, spinach, potatoes and roasted hazelnuts.

TIEN HIANG

Map 5; 14 Rue Bichat, 10th; ///competent.probable.oval; www.tien-hiang.fr

This tiny, family-run spot has been a pioneer of vegan Asian food since the 1990s with its hallmark simple dishes with mesmerizing textures – all inspired by traditional Buddhist cuisine. The "beef", "chicken" and "shrimp" don't sacrifice on taste, so much so that Tien Hiang has become the favourite place for local vegans to convert their sceptical carnivore friends.

L'ABATTOIR VÉGÉTAL

Map 4; 61 Rue Ramey, 18th; ///sobs.remains.volume;
www.abattoirvegetal.com

Few vestiges of this building's past life as an abattoir remain – much to the relief of the meat-free eaters who cross the threshold. It's been given a new lease of life as a flower-filled vegetarian (and sometimes vegan) restaurant, where every dish is made with seasonal, organic ingredients. The brunches tempt everyone to climb up the Butte Montmartre on a weekend, where they're rewarded with vegan matcha pancakes and homemade granola with non-dairy yogurt.

BREATHE RESTAURANT

Map 4; 16 Rue Henry Monnier, 9th; ///tanks.buzz.relaxing;
www.breathe-restaurant.com

You'll need to make a reservation at this trendy modern restaurant, where even carnivores are clamouring to taste the seitan burgers. If your veggie pal is in town at the weekend, skip the classic meals and book for the "tea time" instead to impress them with handmade cakes. Everything is specially designed with coeliacs in mind, too.

SEASON SQUARE

Map 6; 3 Rue Louise Weiss, 13th; ///fencing.luggage.asleep;
www.season-square.com

Don't let the massive concrete pillar at the entrance deter you: Season Square may not look like much, but trust the local devotees when they say this is where you'll find the best vegan burger. The fluffy bun, juicy veggie steak and savvy sauce combination create an elegantly balanced taste. Most of the customers are from the office district nearby, but true vegan gourmets cross the Seine for a taste of the healthy, homemade seasonal cuisine here.

» Don't leave without trying the cinnamon roll, if you're lucky and there's any left. The flavoursome doughy bread is unbeatable.

POTAGER DE CHARLOTTE

Map 4; 12 Rue Louise-Émilie de la Tour d'Auvergne, 9th;
///unstable.dream.campers; www.lepotagerdecharlotte.fr

When it comes to vegan fine dining (once unthinkable in Paris), banish any ideas you have about meat substitutes or meat-free imitations of classic dishes. Instead, in this swish, royal-green dining room, fresh and seasonal cooking reigns supreme. Combinations that sound simple – such as grilled courgettes with a tomato sauce, rice and pesto – are anything but in flavour and appearance. Two brothers are responsible for this kitchen magic, where plates are as colourful and photo-worthy as in any contemporary bistro.

Try it!
PICK UP PLANT-BASED

For ingredients to whip up your own meat-free meal, check out the vegan concept store Aujourd'hui Demain (42 Rue du Chemin Vert, 11th). It stocks vegan clothing and beauty products, too.

BASTILLE

RUE DU FAUBOURG ST-ANTOINE

AVENUE LEDRU ROLLIN

11TH

FAUBOURG
ST-ANTOINE

RUE P. BERT

Indulge in a long lunch at
BISTROT PAUL BERT
This old-school bistro is as
quintessentially Parisian as it
gets. Order the *steak-frites*
– they're the best in the city.

4

Raise a glass at
LE BARON ROUGE
A pre-noon glass of wine is a
Parisian staple. Embrace it
and sip a beautiful Burgundy
at this market-trader haunt.

RUE DE COTTE

RU CROZATIER

RUE DU FAUBOURG ST-ANTOINE

PLACE
MIREILLE
HAVET

3

1 RUE E. CASTELAR

2

Amble through
MARCHÉ D'ALIGRE
Squeeze your way through
the tightly packed stalls of this
market, traders shouting as
they vie for your attention.

Fuel up at
BOULANGERIE BO
Start your day with a
Parisian essential from this
picture-perfect boulangerie:
a croissant still delightfully
warm from the oven.

RUE DE CHARENTON

RUE CHALIGNY

VIADUC DES ARTS

BOULEVARD DIDEROT

RUE

12TH

*Many artisans make up
the **Viaduc des Arts**
community, where a
series of gourmet havens
lie beneath former
railway arches.*

PLACE DU
COLONEL
BOURGOIN

5

BERCY

Get artistic at
ATELIER C
Paris takes its chocolate
seriously. Do the same
and try your hand at a
chocolate-making class,
held in this concept-
store-meets-workshop.

AVENUE DAUMESNIL

0 metres	250
0 yards	250

A morning of
food in the 12th

Parisian food culture is centred on great ingredients – shopping isn't a weekly chore, but a daily joy. In addition to independent fromageries and butchers, every arrondissement has at least one fresh produce market, where stalls are laden with seasonal fruit and vegetables. The Marché d'Aligre is one of the few to open six days a week, and supplies the restaurants nearby with fresh produce and inspiration. There's no more exciting place to be than the 12th, filling tote bags with groceries and dipping into time-honoured haunts.

1. Boulangerie Bo
85 bis Rue de
Charenton, 12th;
01 43 07 75 21
///confined.fault.skews

2. Marché d'Aligre
Place d'Aligre, 12th; www.
marchedaligre.free.fr
///coveted.qualified.readings

3. Le Baron Rouge
1 Rue Théophile Roussel,
12th; www.lebaronrouge.net
///marker.risen.possibly

4. Bistrot Paul Bert
18 Rue Paul Bert, 11th;
01 43 72 24 01
///dragons.held.suitcase

5. Atelier C
123 Avenue Daumesnil, 12th;
www.atelierc.paris
///hits.stewing.outwit

Viaduc des Arts
///deed.rejected.scans

DRINK

Parisians live much of their lives in bars and cafés, where days are spent people-watching from pavement terraces and nights pass conversing with friends over a leisurely tipple.

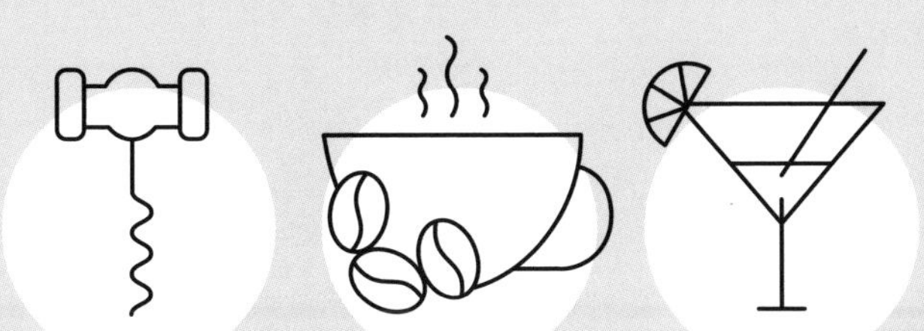

Coffee Shops

When you can lounge on a patio terrace or enjoy the cosy hum of a café, why get your coffee to go? There's nothing like sipping a fresh brew while watching the world go by alongside the locals.

YELLOW TUCAN

Map 2; 20 Rue des Tournelles, 4th; ///zooms.factories.bronzed; www.yellowtucan.com

Around the corner from Place des Vosges is one of the Marais' best-kept secrets for speciality coffee. Owner Vincent is always up for a chat, so students pop in to natter under the pretence of catching up on their reading. With big windows and tables decorated with flowers, it's a calm place to draw breath on a busy day.

CHEZ PRUNE

Map 5; 36 Rue Beaurepaire, 10th; ///start.tools.translate; 01 42 41 30 47

This seemingly prosaic café is a canalside institution. Year after year, everyone shuns the awning-shaded terrace of the latest opening to wait in line for a scuffed metal chair on the pavement here. Stir at least one sugar in your espresso (the only thing to order) and sip it in a cloud of cigarette smoke for a quintessentially Parisian start to the day.

HANOÏ CORNER

Map 4; 7 Rue Blanche, 9th; ///gather.ponies.crew; www. hanoicorner.fr

Given the role France played in bringing coffee to Vietnam, it's surprising that contemporary Vietnamese coffee culture hasn't made greater inroads in Paris. Hoping to change that is this teeny tea room, where dark, intense coffee is served to an in-crowd.

» Don't leave without trying a cup of frothy, tiramisu-esque *café de Hanoi*, a traditional recipe made with eggs and condensed milk.

BACK IN BLACK

**Map 3; 25 Rue Amelot, 11th; ///charm.dilute.pits;
www. backinblackcoffee.com**

There's something almost scientific about the second café-roastery from renowned Parisian coffee pioneers KB. Staff are impeccably smart, measuring out beans and frothing milk with laboratory precision, while hipster patrons wait on restaurant-style seating. The single-origin coffee menu is one of the city's most extensive, and the grilled cheese sandwiches help to calm the stormiest of coffee shakes.

Try it!
BREW A CUP

If you can't get enough of Back in Black's divine brews, you can learn the art of roasting and cupping (coffee tasting) at one of its two-hour workshops. Check the website to find out the latest dates.

Solo, Pair, Crowd

A day in Paris without coffee is simply unthinkable. Get your fix to go or get comfy on a couch indoors.

FLYING SOLO
On the go

Pick up a flat white from Australian-run coffee bar Honor in the 8th to drink as you window-shop along swanky Rue du Faubourg Saint-Honoré.

IN A PAIR
Bath time

If all that walking around town has you exhausted, put your feet up in a claw-foot tub (yep, it doubles as a seat here) and sip on good coffee at Le Pavillon des Canaux, a quirky café in the 19th with the vibe of an eclectic city-centre home.

FOR A CROWD
Coffee with a soundtrack

Stop by community coffee shop and Southeast Asian canteen The Hood in the 11th for a coffee with a banh mi. If you have a musical talent in your midst, there are instruments lying around to be played.

TREIZE AU JARDIN

Map 1; 5 Rue de Médicis, 6th; ///dynamic.jolly.instance;
www.treizeaujardin.com

A real homely feel pervades this Swedish-American-run bakery, from
the warm welcome to its snug nooks. It's a meeting place for the expat
community that have called this area home since the 1920s, but the
Southern hospitality has drawn Paris-born crowds in their droves, too.
>> Don't leave without trying one of the bakery's famous American
classics: a pecan-chocolate cookie to tuck into between coffee sips.

CAFÉOTHÈQUE

Map 2; 52 Rue de l'Hôtel de Ville, 4th; ///tougher.water.moves;
www.lacafeotheque.com

There was once a time when ordering a cappuccino in Paris would
be met with a raised eyebrow – and the quality of a good coffee was
measured in bitterness and strength alone. We have Caféothèque
to thank for paving the way for change. You'll be hard-pressed to
find a Parisian who hasn't whiled away an afternoon cradling a rich
brew at Gloria Monténégro's cosy temple to new-wave coffee.

CAFÉ PIMPIN

Map 4; 64 Rue Ramey, 18th; ///slice.steeped.closets; 01 46 06 97 25

The area around the Sacré-Cœur may no longer be the village it
was in Van Gogh's day, but nearby Jules Joffrin, where this café abides,
is the modern equivalent. Instead of sipping absinthe in bordels and
bars, these days folks catch up over chai lattes in cute spots like this.

Wine Bars

Meeting friends for a glass of wine is the post-work catch-up event of choice. Something to snack on as you drink is customary, whether it's a few almonds or a cheese board to work through into the night.

LA BELLE HORTENSE

Map 2; 31 Rue Vieille du Temple, 3rd; ///fencing.disclose.swinging;
www.cafeine.com/fr/belle-hortense

Merging good books with good wine, this timeless spot is so special that literature lovers can't resist showing it off to friends visiting from abroad. From the moment you set eyes on the vintage indigo-blue

Nestled in the corner of the oldest covered walkway of the city is Coinstot Vino *(22–30 Galerie Montmartre)*, a laid-back bar that is hidden well enough to be missed. Shelves packed with divine elixir reflect an extensive cellar selection, including a substantial organic range. Opt for the "wine by glass" list and savour each sip on the unique interior terrace. Who needs a sommelier for a full winery experience?

façade, its window full of colourful books and a variety of spirits, you're staying put for the night. Inside, regulars engage in debates at the bar while intellectuals sip on fine wine and browse the wooden bookshelves. Blend in with a glass of the "wine of the month", settle on a stool in the cosy space and live the Parisian bohemian dream.

POMPETTE

Map 4; 15 Rue Hippolyte Lebas, 9th; ///readings.polite.dices; www.pompetteparis.com

Many Parisians claim never to have one too many, but at Pompette you're practically encouraged to (elegantly) over-indulge and get a bit tipsy – "pompette" means just that in French. Run by an Australian, French and Canadian team, the 28-seat bar (yes, you'll need to book ahead) has a seriously exciting natural wine list (that's wine made with minimal intervention on a small scale) and a tasty food menu to match.

>> **Don't leave without** trying a bottle of Pet Nat – fizz made by the ancestral method – from Kumpf & Meyer.

DEV!ANT

Map 4; 39 Rue des Petites Écuries, 10th; ///packages.grownup.exam; www.vivantparis.com/deviant

No seats? No problem. There's not a single stool or chair at this mirror-walled bar, open entirely onto the street. Instead, trendy Parisians gather at the slim marble counters, drinking their way through bottles of Rue de la Soif Sauvignon Blanc or unusual Austrian rosés poured by a young team with attitude (and enviable wine knowledge).

MR ALPHONSE

Map 3; 8 Rue de la Folie Méricourt, 11th;
///because.striving.empire; 06 08 73 63 72

When almost every table is booked out on a Friday night, you know you're onto a good thing. With a living-room-style cellar perfect for groups, Mr Alphonse is the father-and-son-run wine bar you wish was at the end of your road. The enormous charcuterie platters are made to share, and there's no unnecessarily encyclopaedic wine list.

FREDDY'S

Map 1; 54 Rue de Seine, 6th; ///mailing.piglet.those; 07 89 29 91 05

There's not a hint of snobbery at this Brooklyn-esque bar with its stone walls, wooden stalls and lively crowd. Those inclined to panic in the presence of haughty sommeliers will find the welcome warm and English spoken, handy given the extensive choice of wines by the glass.

LE BARON ROUGE

Map 3; 1 Rue Théophile Roussel, 12th; ///marker.risen.possibly;
www.lebaronrouge.net

The cheapest thimble-sized glasses of wine in Paris are drunk standing up at barrel tables at this Aligre institution. During the day you'll join traders from the adjacent marché *(p88)*, at night mates enjoying an easy-going *apéro*. There's a wide range of wines listed on chalkboards, but take too long to decide and you'll lose your place in the queue.

» Don't leave without trying a platter of oysters, shucked just outside the bar at the weekend when in season, paired with a glass of Chablis.

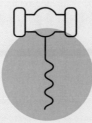

Liked by the locals

"Mr Alphonse is my go-to spot
for an after-work drink or *apéro*.
The wine list is interesting
and diverse, the atmosphere
relaxed and the cheeses delicious
(try my favourite, the burrata
with truffle oil)."

JOCELYN CLARK, WINE GUIDE

Cocktail Joints

While wine is made to be enjoyed with a meal in Paris, cocktails are an art deserving sole attention. Serious mixology is often a special occasion splurge, with only the best bars dedicated to the craft.

BISOU

Map 2; 15 Boulevard du Temple, 3rd;
///gaps.mime.chickens; www.bar-bisou.fr

There's no menu at this self-styled sexy spot, so get chatting to the staff for a drink tailored to your mood and preferences. If €10 creations weren't good enough, all non-alcoholic ingredients are seasonal and sourced in France, and leftover fruits get transformed into garnishes as part of a zero-waste policy.

CAFÉ CHÉRI(E)

Map 5; 44 Boulevard de la Villette, 19th;
///hobbit.upstairs.actor; 09 53 05 93 36

Topping the list of Belleville's social spots is this instantly recognizable red bar, where hip young locals welcome the easy-going vibe and bargain cocktails. Take a seat at one of the classroom-style tables and observe the shifting ambience as if you're at a house party.

DIRTY LEMON

**Map 3; 24 Rue de la Folie Méricourt, 11th; ///napkins.asks.sound;
www.dirtylemonbar.com**

This spot has redefined the cocktail bar, creating a new kind of
female-run and inclusive space that was lacking on the Paris scene.
Turning over-fussy menus on their head with cheekily named drinks
like Soft Butch and Trophy Wife has made Dirty Lemon a firm
stomping ground for groups of girlfriends and an LGBTQ+ clientele.
» Don't leave without trying the Poor Little Rich Girl, a mix of
mezcal, aloe vera, chartreuse and verjus.

GRAVITY BAR

**Map 5; 44 Rue des Vinaigriers, 10th; ///soldiers.valve.massing;
06 98 54 92 49**

Don't be intimidated by the sleek interior and many accolades: the
vibe here is laidback, the kind of place to rock up in your jeans rather
than show off your designer gear. Decide whether you want a drink
that's sweet, bitter or in between and the bartenders will mix it up.

Try it!
SHAKE IT UP

If you've learned a thing or two watching
mixologists, head to speciality spirits shop
Esprit 50cl (*www.esprit50cl.fr*) in the 11th to
pick up unusual French-made spirits to
make your own cocktails at home.

Liked by the locals

"While many Parisians choose to gather at the riverbank to enjoy drinks on sunny days, there really is nothing like sipping a cocktail on the *terrasse* of a Parisian café and gazing at the lively streets."

AGNES BAREILLE, PUBLIC TRANSPORTATION
PROJECT MANAGER

LA COMMUNE

Map 5; 80 Boulevard de Belleville, 20th;
///guessing.modules.petal; www.syndicatcocktailclub.com

Winning cocktail combinations don't get much better than chalice-like punch bowls served to share in a lovely fairy-light-lit, plant-filled conservatory. A tropical vibe pervades here year-round, fuelled by generous ladles of rum punch and a banging hip-hop soundtrack.

LULU WHITE

Map 4; 12 Rue Frochot, 9th; ///minority.bake.herring; www.luluwhite.bar

Almost every kind of late-night revelry can be found on rowdy Rue Frochot, yet it's still somewhat of a surprise to find an authentic New Orleans-inspired speakeasy among the road's drinking dens. This classy spot has prices to match, but a night of Ramos-gin-fizz-fuelled fun awaits. The decor – velvet booths and mirrored ceilings – is a little bit over the top and a little bit luxe, much like the clientele.

>> **Don't leave without** trying an absinthe flight. It's not hallucinogenic like it was during the belle époque, but it still packs a punch.

SHERRY BUTT

Map 2; 20 Rue Beautreillis, 4th; ///saving.pavement.shadow; 09 83 38 47 80

This is the kind of place you stroll to for an end-of-night drink on the way home but end up sticking around until they kick you out (usually around 2am). The reason? The whisky creations, of which the bartenders are passionate advocates, ready to share their insights while they mix you up one of the best old-fashioneds in Paris.

Breweries and Wineries

France has always celebrated its regional wines and beers, but few had been made in Paris until recently. With this change came a raft of exciting new businesses (and excited punters to match).

BRASSERIE DE LA GOUTTE D'OR

Map 4; 28 Rue de la Goutte d'Or, 18th; ///collect.unable.oblige;
www.brasserielagouttedor.com

The beers brewed here may be staples on grocery store shelves across Paris, but nothing beats visiting the brand's taproom, usually open two days a week. Staunch fans come to get the inside scoop from the team – oh, and to brag about being one of the first to taste the latest, locally sourced creations.

LES CUVES DE FAUVE

Map 3; 64 Rue de Charonne, 11th; ///puns.pinches.deny; www.fauvebiere.com

Colourful, fun and free from beer-bro culture, this bright brewpub shows how far the scene has come. On sunny days, drinkers spill out onto the terrace beneath the blue awnings, soaking up the rays and sipping one of the rotating sixteen beers on tap – all brewed on site. If you somehow haven't got your beer fix yet, the burgers and fries come with toppings like reblochon and shallots confited in IPA.

» **Don't leave without** trying the Billet Doux, a light and fresh peach Blanche (also available by the bottle to ship home).

LA VIGNE DE SURESNES
Map 6; 4 Rue du Passage Saint-Maurice, Suresnes;
///booster.fight.liver; 01 42 04 96 75

Just beyond the city limits proper, across the Seine from the Bois de Boulogne, is this bijou winery. But with the Eiffel Tower as the backdrop to the vines, Paris doesn't feel too far away. Scooping awards for its Chardonnay-Sauvignon blends, La Vigne de Suresnes honours the long tradition of great wine made in Suresnes – beloved by monarchs in the 1500s and 1600s. Book a tour and tasting to find out why.

La Winerie Parisienne is the big gun of the Parisian winemaking scene, its bottles appearing on bar menus all over the city. That's not the only way to taste the blends, though. The brand's winery out in Montreuil isn't routinely open to visitors, but its umbrella group, Paris Maison de Vins, also encompasses the Domaine la Bouche du Roi – just outside the city on the Plaine de Versailles, and open for visits. Find out about its latest adventures and tastings at www.winerieparisienne.fr.

PANAME BREWING COMPANY

Map 5; 41 bis Quai de la Loire, 19th; ///implore.lateral.vote;
www.panamebrewingcompany.com

Perhaps the best-known of all the micro-breweries in Paris (thanks to its enormous floating terrace at the top of the Bassin de la Villette), Paname lives up to its hype. With great views over the water and an airy, industrial indoor space, it's popular day and night with large groups of all ages who come to watch the sightseeing boats ply up and down the canal while tasting their way through the pale ales.

» Don't leave without trying the Brexiteer: a delicious IPA (and friendly dig at the Brits) to mark the UK's departure from the EU.

LA FINE MOUSSE

Map 3; 4 bis Avenue Jean Aicard, 11th; ///dragons.inspector.part;
www.lafinemousse.fr

Split into a bar and restaurant facing each other, this spot has all the requisites for serious beer geeks to practically move in. One of the city's original champions of craft beer, La Fine Mousse has built

Try it!
TAKE A BREWERY TOUR

Oberkampf's BAPBAP brewery (*www.bap bap.paris*) in the 11th is one of the few to offer tours in English. They run on Fridays and offer an introduction to the brewing process – as well as a tasting, of course.

a city-wide reputation pouring niche beers from France, Belgium, Sweden and beyond in this pleasing backstreet pocket of the 11th. On the north side is the bar, where a relaxed vibe slowly turns lively as punters test 20 different options on tap (plus many more by the bottle). On the south side is the restaurant, where things get more serious, with a six-course tasting menu waiting to soak up that beer.

VIGNERONS PARISIENS

Map 6; 60 Rue Gay-Lussac, 5th; ///modest.historic.panel; www.lesvignerons.paris

A new entrepreneurial city-centre venture is out to overtake the micro-brewery: the micro-winery. Some 60 years after the last large-scale cellars closed at Bercy, the owners behind this urban winery are bringing winemaking back to the heart of Paris with a whole lot of love. During a tasting session, you'll find out how Matthieu, Emmanuel and Frédéric bring their grapes to Paris and ferment their boutique range of reds and whites in this bijou space. It's one to show off to visiting parents.

BAR GALLIA

Map 6; 35 Rue Méhul, Pantin; ///grain.student.vent; www.galliaparis.com

Even some life-long Parisians have yet to tread outside the city limits to up-and-coming semi-suburb Pantin, where Bar Gallia – of the brewery of the same name – calls home. Those in the know jump on the metro to join everyone from millennials to an older crowd, who congregate in the beer garden on a mission to drink the place dry.

Unmissable Terraces

The **terrasse** *is a Paris institution – so much so that alfresco spots are tough to score on sunny days. Imagine cafés under umbrellas lining cobblestone streets and year-round people-watching. Divine.*

LE PROGRÈS

Map 2; 1 Rue de Bretagne, 3rd; ///dance.teaspoons.special; 08 93 02 53 54

Chattering students and fashion interns fill the tables under the signature red awnings of this corner café. The theme is young and trendy for the most part, but keep an eye open: this place feels plucked out of the 1960s, and some patrons seem like extras in a film. It's a neighbourhood go-to with no-frills coffee and cold beer, and bustling Rue de Bretagne offering up all the entertainment you need.

LE COMPAS D'OR

Map 1; 62 Rue Montorgueil, 2nd; ///cups.senses.unveils;
www.lecompas-restaurant.com

See a table and grab it: there's no use being timid at this oft-crowded favourite. A pitcher of house wine is all you need as you tuck yourself between other patrons for some of the best people-watching along Rue Montorgueil. Friends mingle late into the evening, coming and going as they please, staying until the waiters start bringing in the few dozen chairs and tables to signal the night's end. Just wedge in, get the waiter's attention and make a choice: red or white?

GRANDE MOSQUÉE DE PARIS

Map 6; 47 Rue Geoffroy-Saint-Hillaire, 5th;
///deny.swear.motivations; www.mosqueedeparis.net

So it's not quite on the pavement, but rather in a secluded, leafy courtyard that makes it feel like a true find for those who stumble upon it. Serving up €2 mint tea and North African pastries, the mosque's charming café truly transports you to Morocco. Birds flutter around the tiled tables picking up crumbs, while locals wave for more of the sweet tea and bask in a moment of tranquillity.

» Don't leave without trying the traditional North African pastries flavoured with jasmine and orange-blossom.

COMPTOIR DES ARCHIVES

Map 2; 41 Rue des Archives, 3rd; ///begin.sloping.perform; 01 42 72 13 56

It's hard to miss this corner café when strolling down one of the two major thoroughfares it covers. Walk by in the morning and you'll see regulars stopping by for a quick espresso and some banter before the working day starts; return in the afternoon and it's the haunt of passersby who sip on a mint lemonade and tuck into escargot for lunch. It doesn't try hard, which is why it's become a neighbourhood favourite for a simple drink while taking in the foot traffic on the adjoining Rue des Archives and Rue Rambuteau.

LES PHILOSOPHES CAFÉ

Map 2; 28 Rue Vieille du Temple, 4th; ///release.memory.memory;
www.cafeine.com/en/philosophes

There's something charming about the terrace of this classic French bistro in the winter, when old-timers cosy up in their scarves under outdoor heaters, lingering over a glass of affordable house wine and watching the comings and goings of the colourful Marais district. A selection of proudly homemade small dishes make this an all-day-and-night place to nibble, sip and watch.

LA MARINE

Map 5; 55 bis Quai de Valmy, 10th; ///above.infects.costs;
www.lamarinecanalsaintmartin.com

This archetypical corner café overlooking the Canal Saint-Martin is the kind of place that you pop into for a lunchtime salad and before you know it you're ordering a cognac. It's spruced up in recent years,

Shh!

Coffee shop KB in the 9th (*62 Rue des Martyrs*) is well known to Mac-wielding locals, but as they set up stations inside, the lucky few know the best spot is on the terrace outside. Set back from the traffic, it's perfect for watching all manner of crowds coming up the hilly street. Secure a seat, head in to order, then sip your coffee – it's the good stuff – once it arrives, with a somewhat smug feeling while freelancers work indoors.

with a fully heated terrace in winter, but the waterfront tables are in high demand no matter the season thanks to the perfect side-by-side seating, allowing you to keep chatting with an eye on the foot traffic along the water. The drink menu plays all the greatest hits, tempting you to linger beyond that cognac.

LA PLACE VERTE

Map 3; 105 Rue Oberkampf, 11th; ///palaces.chop.flags; 01 43 57 34 10

Large terraces are so rare in this district that those in the know rush to claim a table here on sunny days before everyone else cottons on. An official street art project takes up space on the corner, providing an authentic urban backdrop to constant chatter and spirited laughter in the air, courtesy of cutting-edge creatives. The wall art is renewed bi-monthly, should you need an excuse to return.

GRAND MARCHÉ STALINGRAD

Map 5; 6–8 Place de la Bataille de Stalingrad, 19th;
///mondays.liberty.crowned; www.arotondestalingrad.com

Far from the tourist draws, this remnant of the old city wall is home to an expansive terrace. As soon as summer hits, young professionals pack into lounge chairs under umbrellas to sip a mojito and mingle. It's the people you meet who shape a visit at this atmospheric terrace, where it always feels like Saturday night no matter the time of day.

» Don't leave without trying a kebab from the Mediterranean food kiosk that sets up a stand on the adjacent square. They're gourmet, and a step up from the usual street-side vendors in Paris.

Settle in at
MARLUSSE ET LAPIN

Snag one of the swing seats at this dive bar where bohemians hang out in Montmartre today (absinthe sometimes included).

18TH

BLVD DE LA CHAPELLE

*In the early 20th century, many people visited the **Moulin Rouge** for easily obtainable absinthe and opium as much as for the shows.*

BLVD DE CLICHY

③

RUE BLANCHE

PIGALLE

RUE CONDORCET

BOULEVARD

RUE DU FAUBOURG ST-DENIS

9TH

8TH

SQUARE DE LA TRINITÉ

LA FAYETTE

RUE D'HAUTEVILLE

DE

MAGENTA

10TH

Step back in time at
HARRY'S NEW YORK BAR

Get cosy in this wood-panelled bar, where the French 75 and the Bloody Mary were invented. Order one for you and the other for your pal.

RUE

LA

BLVD HAUSSMANN

Get in the spirit at
LE SYNDICAT

Get a taste of contemporary cocktail culture at this innovative bar, where old-fashioned French spirits are revived in unique concoctions.

④

PL DE L'OPÉRA

②

2ND

①

BLVD ST-MARTIN

RUE DE TURBIGO

3RD

Learn the secrets at
THE RITZ

Splash out on a masterclass in cocktail-making – and delve into the lives of the Ritz's illustrious guests – with Colin Peter Field.

Bar Hemingway
is named in the writer's honour – a place where he drank 51 martinis in a row to celebrate Paris's liberation after WWII.

BLVD DE SÉBASTOPOL

MARAIS

7TH

INVALIDES

BOULEVARD

La Seine

4TH

RUE

DE

RIVOLI

ST-GERMAIN

6TH

Île de la Cité

BOULEVARD

RASPAIL

LATIN QUARTER

Île St-Louis

5TH

0 metres 500
0 yards 500

An evening of
cocktail culture

Wine may be the tipple most associated with Paris, but many great cocktails (sidecar, mimosa, rose) were born here. Paris is, after all, where some of the world's most talented (and troubled) artists spent nights fuelled by absinthe, and where the "Lost Generation" partied so hard that Parisians have spent another two generations trying to recreate their excesses. Though the city is by no means trapped in the 1920s, you can't sip cocktails in the 2020s without travelling through a century of serious mixology – just pace yourself.

1. The Ritz
15 Place Vendôme, 1st;
www.ritzescoffier.com
///video.fuzzy.ticked

2. Harry's New York Bar
5 Rue Daunou, 2nd;
www.harrysbar.fr
///bliss.qualified.approve

3. Marlusse et Lapin
14 Rue Germain Pilon, 18th;
01 42 59 17 97
///brighter.success.bunkers

4. Le Syndicat
51 Rue du Faubourg Saint-Denis, 10th; www.syndicat
cocktailclub.com
///sifts.retrain.bright

5. Moonshiner
5 Rue Sedaine, 11th;
www.moonshinerbar.fr
///apron.sang.youthful

Bar Hemingway
///compiled.edges.opens

Moulin Rouge
///enforced.lakes.sling

BLVD DE LA VILLETTE

BLVD RICHARD LENOIR

PLACE DE LA RÉPUBLIQUE

BLVD DU TEMPLE

11TH

BLVD BEAUMARCHAIS

Nightcap at MOONSHINER
Push open the fridge inside Pizza Da Vito and enter Paris's first speakeasy: a dimly lit, jazz-playing bar.

PL. DE LA BASTILLE

BASTILLE

SHOP

Scouting the best produce at an open-air market, designing your own scent, hunting for one-of-a-kind outfits – shopping is one of life's simple pleasures in Paris.

Gourmet Treats

Foodie fans with a finesse for fine dining, Parisians are never short of quality produce in their cuisine. Specialist gourmet shops are the place to go in search of delicious ingredients and edible gifts.

CONFITURE PARISIENNE

Map 3; 17 Avenue Daumesnil, 12th; ///angle.dished.locating; www.confiture-parisienne.com

Though Parisians rarely eat breakfast (many just survive on a strong shot of coffee), when they do, they do it in style. Join the preserve connoisseurs and peruse the quirky flavours of jam (carrot and vanilla anyone?) in this high-end shop under the arches of the Coulée Verte. Invest in a pretty pot and you're sure to make any home brunch boujee.

Try it!
JAM FROM SCRATCH

Got a serious sweet tooth? Book a spot at one of Confiture Parisienne's monthly jam-making classes. You'll find out some of their secrets and leave with your own personalized jar to take home.

MAISON PLISSON

Map 2; 93 Boulevard Beaumarchais, 3rd; ///grin.spent.dented;
www.lamaisonplisson.com

This beloved luxury food hall offers a gourmet shopping experience like no other. Upstairs you'll find locally produced veg, meat and cheese, while downstairs is a gold mine of jars, tins and bottles to take home. It's pricey, but foodies will tell you it's worth it.

» **Don't leave without** buying a few of their smart "tartinables" to spread on toast for *apéro*: the truffled artichoke cream is a knock-out.

TAKA & VERMO

Map 5; 61 bis Rue du Faubourg Saint-Denis, 10th;
///dine.fakes.stuffing; 01 48 24 89 29

While doing their weekly shop, locals often pop by this artisan cheese store for a special treat. The cheese here is sustainably sourced and hand-selected by its young owners, Laure Takahashi and Mathieu Vermorel – self-confessed fromage fanatics. It's a lovely little place to grab some treats for a picnic in nearby Jardin Villemin.

LE VIN AU VERT

Map 4; 70 Rue de Dunkerque, 9th; ///steadily.rocky.flow; 01 83 56 46 93

A wine shop by day and restaurant at dinner, Le Vin au Vert is a popular destination among wine sellers and makers, renowned for its natural wines and generous Jura allocations. Set between the insalubrious streets around Barbès and the pretty Square d'Anvers, it's the kind of place you'll only stumble upon if you come searching.

E. DEHILLERIN

Map 1; 18–20 Rue Coquillière, 1st; ///slippers.alarmed.glow;
www.edehillerin.fr

If Ratatouille were to go kitchenware shopping in Paris, he'd head to
E. Dehillerin. This is the city's temple to cookware, and reverence is
wholly encouraged. With few visible prices and little signage, it's near
impossible to navigate and can be ruinously expensive – but standing
perplexed beneath the towering racks of plush pans is all part of the
experience. Top tip: the sturdy copper pans will last a lifetime.

BMK

Map 5; 14 Rue de la Fidélité, 10th; ///funded.silly.panthers;
www.bmkparis.com

Come lunch or dinner, cool young couples and vegan friends head to
this hipster hangout for some of Paris's best African cuisine. There's a
small *épicerie* (grocery) hidden here, too, where you can pick up some
of the ingredients that make BMK's homemade dishes so delicious.
The products change seasonally and are based on availability,
ranging from tamarind jam to organic Ethiopian coffee. Pop by to
pick up a gift and you'll probably find yourself staying for some food.

VELAN

Map 5; 87 Passage Brady, 10th; ///buck.gangs.passages; www.velan.paris

This beloved grocery store has been a fixture inside Passage Brady
(p182), a centre for local Indian and Pakistani communities, for forty
years and has a wide fanbase to show for it. Initiated regulars come to

this treasure trove to stock up on different kinds of pepper, cassava, chutneys and a host of spices to amplify the flavours in their dishes. There's no better stop for authentic Indian specialties.

A LA VILLE DE RODEZ

Map 2; 22 Rue Vieille du Temple, 4th; ///bridges.uptown.spreads; 01 48 87 79 36

As the rest of the Marais has gentrified, it's a testament to the quality of A la Ville de Rodez's products that this deli has changed little over the past hundred years – *saucissons* still dangle from the ceiling and window displays are laden with pâté. It's been family-run for generations (they live upstairs) and their passion for regional produce is shared by their loyal clientele, many of whom will give you tips on what to buy.

» **Don't leave without** buying a slice of St Nectaire, an earthy, washed-rind cheese that's one of the best specialities of the Auvergne.

Shh!

Stop by Edwart Chocolatier (*www.edwart.fr*) in the Marais and ask to try some sugary samples. It doesn't advertise this, but you're welcome to taste the jewel-like creations (the curry praline chocolate is a great choice). Chocolate maker Edwin Yansané, often working the counter, is as friendly as his products are magical. Consider buying a box of ganaches or one of the fantastic chocolate spreads, including a salted caramel sauce that likely won't survive the journey home.

Beloved Markets

*Outdoor and covered markets are the cornerstone
of local life, with one gracing every arrondissement.
Whether it's for bric-a-brac, vintage items or fresh
produce, remember to bring a canvas bag (or five).*

MARCHÉ D'ALIGRE

**Map 3; Place d'Aligre, 12th; ///reclaim.dabbled.alarmed;
www.marchedaligre.free.fr**

You can't beat this one. You just can't. This stretch of outdoor food stalls, a covered indoor hall and an adjacent flea market opens six days a week. On Saturday and Sunday mornings, join the crush of Parisians with their caddies and canvas bags as they do their weekly produce shopping. Sellers shout the day's deals as customers grab and bag their own fruit and vegetables. If ever there were a place to get pushed away by an older Parisian woman, this is it.

MARCHÉ PRÉSIDENT-WILSON

Map 6; Avenue du Président Wilson, 16th; ///silently.magical.many

By virtue of its location in a ritzy district, this twice-weekly open-air market is where you'll find the most gourmet of Parisians. Renowned Michelin star chefs order their seasonal vegetables here and chichi

Follow the chefs to Rungis, Europe's largest wholesale market in the suburbs, where restaurants source their food. locals come to pick up refined supplies for their dinner parties. It's not a pretentious affair, though: the vendors are as joyful as their colourful stalls, tempting customers with tasting platters and a side of banter.

MARCHÉ SAINT-PIERRE

Map 4; 2 Rue Charles Nodier, 18th; ///empty.spiking.fired; www.marchesaintpierre.com

Fancy making some cool new cushion covers? Always wanted to design your own fashion line? In the shadow of the Sacré-Cœur, this warren-like complex, spread out over six floors, seems to feature every fabric in the world to get you started. The couturiers and student seamstresses who venture inside always leave with a few metres for a home décor or fashion project.

MARCHÉ SAINT-MARTIN

Map 5; 20 Rue Bouchardon, 10th; ///returns.remind.supply

This humble covered market doesn't usually make it into the guides, but to overlook it would be a shame. Here, English exists in rare whispers among accidental tourists who wander in from the nearby Eurostar terminal at Gare du Nord. Moving swiftly past them are easy-going locals, who dip into German grocery boutiques and pick up fresh flowers during their work breaks.

» **Don't leave without** buying a portion of freshly churned salted butter and tangy goat cheeses from the artisan cheese vendor.

MARCHÉ BIOLOGIQUE DES BATIGNOLLES

Map 4; 34 Boulevard des Batignolles, 8th; ///protect.discount.quibble

Buying bio – aka organic – borders on an obsession in Paris. Save yourself the trouble of hopping from greengrocer to deli and stop by this Saturday food market instead. Will you find a bargain in this increasingly desirable neighbourhood? Absolutely not. Shopping here is a post-espresso and pre-exhibition weekend event, where you're more likely to find couples strolling hand in hand, perhaps picking up imported Spanish ham or artisanal honey, than determined queue-jumpers fighting over the best frisée lettuce.

VILLAGE SAINT-PAUL

**Map 2; 20 Rue Saint-Paul, 4th; ///charted.able.decoder;
www.levillagesaintpaul.com**

This calm tangle of courtyards, tucked between the Marais and the Seine, houses antique stores, a hat maker and even a shop dedicated to locally sourced inventions. Village Saint-Paul mercifully lacks the stress of the more popular shopping venues, providing an oasis for browsing shops without pressure. There's a friendly, community vibe to it all, where chatting with a shopkeeper as you browse artisan wallpaper and a bit of haggling with the dealers is all to be expected. And with a few laidback cafés to settle into when the shopping is done, it's hard not to love this little enclave.

» Don't leave without checking the schedule to time your visit with a *brocante* or *vide grenier*, flea markets that pop up here once a month and see pedlars lay their wares on outdoor tables.

MARCHÉ DEJEAN

Map 4; Rue Dejean, 18th; ///purses.neutron.pints

Strong spices and fishy aromas met with the sounds of vendors bartering and residents chatting away envelope you as soon as you hit the area known as "Little Africa". A North and West African community has lived in the Goutte d'Or neighbourhood for decades (hence the nickname), and this market exists as a hub for these residents. Families and friends come here to socialize while they shuffle between the generously brimming stalls, stocking up on ingredients that they won't find anywhere else – bissap, tiof, manioc, igname and gombo, to name a few – that are essential for making traditional African dishes. This market isn't prettified for tourists, and it can get busy at the best of times, but that's what makes it a real snapshot of local life.

MARCHÉ AUX PUCES DE LA PORTE DE VANVES

Map 6; Avenue Georges Lafenestre, 14th; ///surviving.unto.bubbles; www.pucesdevanves.fr

No matter the weather, bargain hunters descend on the city's most lively flea market, spread over two avenues, every weekend. Breezy traders set up shop on wonky tables early, awaiting the French celebs and niche collectors who bargain with them over a seemingly endless variety of odds and ends. Arrive early, bring cash and remember a few sturdy tote bags – with stalls selling centuries-old folk art, antique perfume bottles and so much more, you're likely to leave with a mish-mash of treasures after spending a few hours at this Aladdin's Cave.

Home Touches

Parisians may have notoriously tiny apartments, but their desire for style means they still devour a good concept or homeware store. Pop by one to pick up your own chic piece of Paris to bring home.

SERGEANT PAPER

Map 5; 26 Rue du Château d'Eau, 10th; ///tangible.clots.mincing;

www.sergeantpaper.com

Follow in the footsteps of the city's young aesthetes and upgrade your home with some funky limited-edition prints from Sergeant Paper. This pop art boutique and gallery is a hotspot for art graduates and upcoming illustrators (you may even spot some proud patrons gazing up at their own art on display). Bag one of over 900 original and

Try it!
CREATE A CANDLE

You can channel self-care while caring for the environment on a vegan candle-making course with maker Justine. Search for her course details on www.wecandoo.fr.

affordable – prices start at just two figures – artworks to pop on your wall and you may just pass as Parisian. Your purchased print comes with a certificate of authenticity so you can brag to your pals.

LA TRÉSORERIE

Map 5; 11 Rue du Château d'Eau, 10th; ///debate.belong.meanest; www.latresorerie.fr

Design-forward Parisians happy to splash a bit of cash on functional, albeit very pretty, homeware come here for the crockery, glassware and textiles. A third of products are made in France and the rest in Europe, so there's a hint of sustainability in all of it too. Chances are you'll find something useful for around the house – perhaps in a new aesthetic you never knew you really embodied (Paris can do that).

» Don't leave without ordering a coffee at the adjacent café, which serves up great Swedish-inspired brew, pastries and tartines.

FLEUX'

Map 2; 52 Rue Sainte-Croix de la Bretonnerie, 4th; ///monopoly.occurs.edits; www.fleux.com

No local studio is complete without a set of espresso cups or plant pots from this Marais-born homeware emporium. Fleux's aesthetic is hard to pinpoint and it's anything but understated. You'll find everything here: handmade ceramics, table linens, beeswax wraps, novelty socks and quirky printed totes (perfect for showing off when you pick up your groceries). If you're looking for muted colours and classic French design, head elsewhere: Fleux' is big on personality.

MERCI

Map 2; 111 Boulevard Beaumarchais, 3rd; ///skewed.warriors.drum; www.merci-merci.com

Ask any Parisian who the *crème de la crème* of homeware design is and they're bound to name Merci. The *grand magasin* of concept stores may have spawned a number of offshoot concepts, but it's always important to honour the original. It's also got a healthy conscience, actively funding educational projects in Madagascar.

» Don't leave without taking a break in the café filled with countless second-hand books that you can leaf through (it's one of three on site).

CSAO

Map 2; 9 Rue Elzevir, 3rd; ///coverage.driving.lofts; www.csao.fr

Truly homemade products are hard to come by in Paris, but head to Csao and you'll be spoilt for choice. This shop stocks colourful, ethically created homeware and décor, all individually crafted by West African artisans. Yes they carry a certain price tag, but you'll feel good knowing proceeds go back to social projects in Senegal.

AILLEURS

Map 3; 12 Rue Saint Nicolas, 12th; ///spokes.studio.shocking; www.ailleurs-paris.com

Looking to achieve that rustic French look in your kitchen? Tablescapes and stylized glassware are just a few of the items that line this concept shop. The owner is a graduate of Merci, so the pedigree is reliable – as the design elite who pensively browse the tasteful items will vouch for.

Liked by the locals

"People should visit our boutique because it's a trip to West Africa in the heart of the Marais – a trip in colours and patterns, full of gaiety."

ONDINE SAGLIO, CO-OWNER OF CSAO

Books and Stationery

Every creative dreams of living out a humble existence in Paris. Scribbling away in a notebook on a pavement terrace or dipping into a French novel underneath stacked shelves is as bohemian as it gets.

LIBRAIRIE GALIGNANI

Map 1; 224 Rue de Rivoli, 1st; ///fleet.ribs.brains; www.galignani.fr

Since opening in 1801, this store – which claims to be the continent's oldest English bookshop – has developed a reputation as Paris's most "serious" nook. Despite its prestigious accolades, it's a friendly spot to get lost in. Expect to see booksellers climbing ladders to reach the highest shelf for customers, bibliophiles pondering a purchase in a leather armchair and the odd author hosting a talk.

PAPIER PLUS

Map 2; 9 Rue Pont Louis Philippe, 4th; ///soup.slipped.dogs; www.papierplus.com

The art of letter writing and journaling is alive and well in France, and this pretty store gives Parisians all the more reason to continue that tradition. Since 1976, Papier Plus has been designing stationery for serious writers, as well as those who want you to think they're serious. The minimalist items seem deceptively simple, but these are the little black dresses of paper products; investment pieces that will never fail you. The formats of the timeless monochromatic notebooks haven't changed, but the colours evolve over time, meaning there's something different to tempt you at every visit.

» **Don't leave without** buying the signature *carnet*. Moleskins are available everywhere, but these locally created notebooks aren't.

LIBRAIRIE JOUSSEAUME

**Map 1; 45 Galerie Vivienne, 2nd; ///starred.spot.bucket;
www.librairie-jousseaume.fr**

Galerie Vivienne *(p180)*, restored to its 19th-century glory, seems all the more historical with this old-world bookshop at its heart. Forgotten by locals who only remember it's there when wandering the covered passage, the rickety store survives despite a lack of notoriety. Browse rare history and poetry titles while scaling the winding staircase or opt for cheaper titles on racks in the gallery.

PRÉSENCE AFRICAINE

**Map 2; 25 bis Rue des Écoles, 5th; ///form.sugar.promises;
www.presenceafricaine.com**

The Latin Quarter seems to have a bookstore for every proclivity, and this visionary shop is one not to overlook. Part of a publishing house founded in 1949 to represent African authors, the store stocks fiction and non-fiction that amplify Black voices from Francophone Africa, so maybe skip Victor Hugo for a moment and try something new.

LES MOTS À LA BOUCHE

Map 3; 37 Rue Saint-Ambroise, 11th; ///patting.spin.weds;
www.motsbouche.com

Though gentrification ousted the city's only LGBTQ+ bookshop from its home in the Marais in 2020, it wasn't long before it reopened just outside the district, where it continues to act as a hub of gay and lesbian life. Whatever you're after – art, history, fiction, biography – you'll find it here, and if you can't, just ask the approachable staff. They love to chat about the unique stock and their favourite books.

PAPIER TIGRE

Map 2; 5 Rue des Filles du Calvaire, 11th;
///gravest.openings.lemmings; www.papiertigre.fr

Parisians have long had a love affair with all things Japanese (think Monet and his water lilies), and this Tokyo-born stationery shop is just the latest love note – pun intended. Everything stocked here is

Shh!

Iconic Anglophone bookstore Shakespeare and Company *(www.shakespeareandcompany. com)* may be somewhat of a victim of its own success, but Parisians don't avoid this Left Bank stalwart on that account.

Rather, they bypass the crowds during the day and mingle with local book lovers at niche Sunday events that many tourists don't know about, like feminist book clubs, embroidery sessions and jazz on the terrace outside.

design-forward, from the notebooks with bold geometric patterns to the brightly coloured pencils. Once you've chosen your tools, all that's left to do is find a cute café to start that new writing project.

L'EAU ET LES RÊVES

Map 5; 9 Quai de l'Oise, 19th; ///loosed.lunch.tender;
www.penichelibrairie.com

Parisians will tell you that two of their most beloved pastimes are reading and lounging by the water. L'Eau et les Rêves was onto a good thing, then, when it opened over a decade ago as a floating bookshop on the Canal de l'Ourcq. The barge stocks plenty of nature and travel titles (a nod to the shop's nautical origins) and also hosts intimate readings with upcoming French authors.

» Don't leave without having a coffee and a cake break aboard the boat. Your patronage helps keep this venue afloat (ahem).

THE RED WHEELBARROW

Map 1; 9 Rue de Médicis, 6th; ///puffed.riper.limit;
www.theredwheelbarrowbookstore.com

Locals and expats were devastated when owner Penelope closed up shop in 2012, but six years later she found a fitting home for her English-language bookstore on the Left Bank – the original hub for writers like Hemingway and Gertrude Stein. Though avid Anglophone readers passing through Paris come for the stock, they can't resist staying for Penelope's charm, where a conversation always leads her to pair you with a book you never knew you were looking for.

Street Style

Fancy heels and button-up shirts are mandates from yesteryear's Paris. Ditch the uniforms. Today, Parisians dress for comfort with a vintage flair of their own, mixing chic and casual, sporty and dressy.

SHINZO

Map 1; 23 Rue Étienne Marcel, 1st; ///hook.wink.kitchen; www.shinzo.paris/fr

The launch of a new brand of slick sneakers here is a notoriously big event: walk past on a trainer's national release day and you'll see a crowd of coolly clad sportswear aficionados lining up outside the store, eager to grab the latest offerings. From running shoes to

Paris may be hot on *haute couture*, but you don't need to pay premium prices for designer gear. Skip the Champs-Élysées and head to the 6th instead for consignment store heaven. Chercheminippes *(www.cher cheminippes.fr)* is a mecca for secondhand designer pieces like Louboutin bags and Jimmy Choo shoes – in great condition.

urban footwear, this concept store covers every sports discipline, across five branches on the same road. Expect a suitably snazzy décor in each store: Shinzo are pros at the art of staging premium products, just stop by Shinzo Basketball to see their shrine to the NBA.

LESS IS MORE

Map 5; 22 Rue des Vinaigriers, 10th; ///harps.good.take; 09 52 70 87 60

The eco-conscious crowd swerve fast-fashion promoters and retreat to the comforting corners of this calming boutique, a stone's throw from Canal Saint-Martin. Owner Laetitia has shed all the frivolous packaging and only stocks items produced by eco-friendly manufacturers. You'll find a bit of everything: organic products, capsule collections, cute homewares. The vintage section, however, is the must-see area – bag one of the iconic blue work jumpsuits and you'll be the talk of the town.

FAGUO

Map 2; 81 Rue Vieille du Temple, 3rd; ///become.anchors.spice; www.faguo-store.com/en

Glance down when you're strolling the streets of Paris and you'll probably spot someone wearing a pair of Faguo's tennis shoes – they're on the verge of becoming iconic. This carbon-positive brand is a favourite among millennials, who head here after work for a browse, knowing that for every item they purchase, this young and super-sustainable brand will plant a tree in a forest in France.

» Don't leave without buying a pair of shoes, distinguishable by the button sewn on the heel – they're France's answer to Converse.

ROUJE

**Map 1; 11 bis Rue Bachaumont, 2nd; ///laser.round.brothers;
www.rouje.com**

Imagine a charming Parisian flat bathed in warm lighting with
refined flower arrangements, puffed-up sofas and nostalgic-looking
photos adorning its walls. Wander over to Rue Bachaumont and
you'll find this stylish paradise. Created by model-influencer Jeanne
Damas, Rouje is one of the most *en vogue* local fashion dens.
Join the young fashionistas in this pretty store to browse weekly
releases of selected, innovative items and the occasional surprise
capsule collection. One thing's for sure: you'll always find the French
wardrobe essentials 1970s icon Jane Birkin loved so dearly. Think
sober floaty dresses, old-school denim and chic it-girl bags; paired
with red lipstick and oh-so-casually-styled tousled hair and you've
got the look of "La Parisienne".

» Don't leave without indulging in some delectable seasonal cuisine
and fine wine (or good coffee if it's still a little early) at Chez Jeanne,
the intimate bistro attached to Rouje.

KILIWATCH

Map 1; 64 Rue Tiquetonne, 2nd; ///take.bigger.crawled; www.kiliwatch.paris

Be prepared to trawl through 600 square metres of quirky clothes
at this cool-kid emporium. The size of this spot may seem a bit
overwhelming at first but fear not, this is no ordinary vintage store:
ready-to-wear collections are arranged by colour, style and type.
Come the weekend, you'll see herds of hipsters hunting for a last-
minute party outfit while vintage thrifters root through the rails for

A classic, chic scarf is one of the few clichés the French can't help but still embrace. Pick up a few at Kiliwatch and pay by the kilo.

loud 1980s shirts, vintage Moschino and classic Levi's denim. Whatever your style, it's probably here and though it's a tad pricey, it's worth it when you excavate a truly unique treasure.

MAD LORDS
Map 1; 316 Rue Saint-Honoré, 1st; ///warmers.rash.kebab; www.madlords.com

It's a bit of a treasure hunt finding this unisex jewellery store. Locate the wooden door, tucked away on a boutique-y street, and you'll be taken to a paved courtyard – on the other side of the courtyard lie the jewels. Shimmering from their displays, these heavy pieces are made for stacking and pairing with a couture leather jacket (à la Lenny Kravitz, who's a regular here). You'll have to have a fair bit of cash to splash if you're thinking of investing, but it's still a nice place to browse.

ISAKIN
Map 4; 9 Rue André del Sarte, 18th; ///curl.shampoo.spray; www.isakinparis.com

Thomas Traoré and his crew step up the Parisian street-style game with this exclusive "Made in Paris" brand. They preach comfortable, cool and sustainable menswear, primarily manufactured in local workshops with fabrics sourced from luxury upcycling. They've garnered a solid fanbase among urbanites, particularly for their best-selling graphic T-shirts (they're limited edition, so don't wait around).

Beauty Buys

"Make it simple and natural" is the ultimate motto for French beauty. Parisians maintain their ageless glow by tailoring their own perfect care routine from all the best products.

LIQUIDES BAR À PARFUM

**Map 2; 9 Rue de Normandie, 3rd; ///trash.defended.sublet;
www.liquides-parfums.com**

Parisians don't wait for the trends, they make them. This stylish shop's curated selection of little-known fragrances is like a cocktail bar for your nose (it even looks like a swanky drinks den inside). Just tell the person behind the counter what you're looking for, and they'll serve it up, even requiring you to wear a scent for a bit before

Try it!
SHAPE YOUR SCENT

Paris is practically the capital of perfume, so it's pretty mandatory to spend a couple of hours making your own at the Musée du Parfum's perfumer's workshop *(www.musee-parfum-paris.fragonard.com)*.

committing. Prices might be steep, but these long-lasting, quality products are worth it. Friends' eyes will roll when they ask where you got your fragrance and you say, "Oh, Paris," but you'll love it.

HUYGENS

Map 2; 24 Rue du Temple, 4th; ///openings.rush.ember; www.huygens.fr
A hit of lavender and eucalyptus arouse your senses upon stepping into this tiny boutique. Fittingly housed inside a former apothecary's home, Huygens is all about custom-made cosmetics. Take a whiff of each essential oil blend from the glass jars, then watch as the team infuses your choice into a soap or moisturizer. While you wait for your products, check out the cruelty-free candles, diffusers and other home aromatherapy goods that are proudly made in France – they're great for gifts (or just for spoiling yourself).
» Don't leave without buying a hand cream infused with the essential oils of your choice. Everyone needs a bit of luxury, right?

OH MY CREAM!

Map 1; 104 Rue du Bac, 7th; ///dusts.fire.stadium; www.ohmycream.com
If you feel the need to change up your routine but don't know where to start, let the super-friendly, knowledgeable counsellors at this beloved store guide you. You'll want to buy everything you set your eyes on, but the staff have an unparalleled knowledge and will only let you leave with products that suit your needs and skin type. There are no over-hyped products with unnecessary chemicals here; it's all about clean beauty and effective items from ethical brands.

NOSE

Map 1; 20 Rue Bachaumont, 2nd; ///stripped.candy.index;
www.noseparis.com

The name of this modern boutique says it all, really: let your sense of smell guide you and you'll leave with your perfect scent. This pretty apothecary-esque space takes perfumery all very seriously with its personalized olfactory diagnoses. Coquettish locals rave about the fun shopping experience, where you're encouraged to take a seat at the fragrance bar (typically with a coffee) and get chatting to the expert "noses" who question you on everything from your favourite smells to what you expect from a perfume. What follows is a prescription of sorts as the beauty experts trawl the shelves of branded bottles to find a few scents that suit your tastes. Save yourself the fuss of trailing around countless perfumeries and find that final invisible touch to your Parisian style.

THE NAKED SHOP

Map 3; 75 Rue Oberkampf, 11th; ///altering.lance.prompting;
www.thenakedshop.fr

Packaging-free bulk cosmetics were nowhere to be found in the city until this head-to-toe eco-friendly shop opened. Liquid goods like shampoo, soaps and washing detergent are all sold by weight thanks to self-service dispensers, which encourage you to bring your own container or purchase a glass bottle that you can use time and again (and even return for reimbursement). The palm-free and preservative-free products are all made in France, too, so whether you're filling up with newcomer Ciment or pioneer soaperie Marius

Join the crowds and check out the discount sales at CityPharma for more bulk buys. It's worth it.

Fabre, there's plenty to sweeten your bathroom aroma and conscience. Bulk-buying has never been so chic, and switching to zero waste never so easy.

L'OFFICINE UNIVERSELLE BULY

Map 1; 45 Rue de Saintonge, 3rd; ///sleeper.return.promote; www.buly1803.com/fr

This trademark brand may be globally renowned, but the Marais boutique is one of a kind. It characterizes the charm of an area once inhabited by aristocrats, where dark wooden furniture, antique-style packaging and a replica of the 19th-century Grand Café Torton inside transport you to another era. The vintage products are the kind you'll want to keep even when empty to embellish your bathroom.

» Don't leave without buying a Superfin soap, which you can get customized with a golden vintage monogram, fit for royalty.

LOOX

Map 4; 15 Rue Vignon, 8th; ///research.bagels.shell; www.store.looxwb.com

Looking for the next big thing to add to your clean beauty cupboard? This minimalist concept store has you covered. Sure, you could stop in to restock your skincare supplies with classics from Dermalogica, but it's much more fun to pop caps on testers of French Girl body oils or sample a spritz of an unusual scent like Tobali's Smoke Flower. Many of the products are vegan and cruelty-free, so other than denting your bank balance, there's no need to feel guilty about a splurge.

Rifle through VALOIS VINTAGE

Indulge a serious label obsession at this second-hand store, where a few hundred euros might snag you a pair of Prada flats or some Celine sunglasses.

BOULEVARD DE COURCELLES

PLACE CHARLES DE GAULLE

AVENUE DE FRIEDLAND

BLVD HAUSSMANN

BLVD MALESHERBES

AVENUE DES CHAMPS ÉLYSÉES

Pay homage at MUSÉE YVES SAINT LAURENT

Walk the halls of the chic atelier where YSL designed his collections from 1974 to 2002, now a museum covering his life and work.

8TH

AVE MATIGNON

3

RUE DE SURÈNE

PLACE DE LA MADELEINE

2

1

AVE MONTAIGNE

Window-shop along AVENUE MONTAIGNE

Take a stroll down the glitziest avenue in Paris, pausing at Chanel, Givenchy and Dior.

AVE DE PRÉSIDENT WILSON

PLACE DE LA CONCORDE

16TH

The Flame of Liberty, an unofficial memorial to Princess Diana, stands near **Pont d'Alma***, where the fashion icon died in 1997.*

La Seine

BLVD DE LA TOUR MAUBOURG

INVALIDES

7TH

BOULEVARD

AVENUE DE SUFFREN

BOULEVARD DES INVALIDES

AVENUE DE SÉGUR

0 metres	500
0 yards	500

An afternoon of
haute couture

Paris is considered the world's fashion capital for a reason. French style is synonymous with household names (Chanel, Dior, Louis Vuitton), but beyond these international juggernauts, there's so much more — not least the artists whose labels only later became runway staples. Avoid the Champs-Élysées proper — now the domain of chain shops and fast-food joints — and explore the surrounding streets, where consignment stores hold designer pieces at a fraction of the price and shops elevate clothing into a fine art.

Become an artisan at L'ÉCOLE DES ARTS JOAILLIERS
Book a hands-on, two-hour introduction to enamelling techniques at Van Cleef & Arpels' prestigious jewellery school.

9TH

2ND

PLACE VENDÔME

RUE D. CASANOVA

AVE DE L'OPÉRA

RUE DE RIVOLI

1ST

The arcades of the **Palais Royal** *have been the perfect runway setting for fashion-week shows from the likes of Louis Vuitton.*

ST-GERMAIN

6TH

1. Musée Yves Saint Laurent
5 Avenue Marceau, 16th;
www.museeyslparis.com
///helm.square.wishing

2. Avenue Montaigne
Avenue Montaigne, 8th
///masters.large.nibbles

3. Valois Vintage
8 Rue des Saussaies, 8th; www.valois
vintage-paris.com
///mashing.nurse.touchy

4. L'École des Arts Joailliers
31 Rue Danielle Casanova, 1st; www.le
colevancleefarpels.com
///vampire.coached.simply

📍 **Pont d'Alma** ///modes.zips.obstruction

📍 **Palais Royal** ///smoking.copycat.caller

ARTS & CULTURE

Paris is shaped by its cultural landscape, which honours the masters of the past, admires the innovators of today and inspires the change-makers of tomorrow.

Museum Lates

Let tour groups, school children and chattering families take over the museums during the day. At night, these hubs belong to the adults, who get a post-work culture fix with the odd concert thrown in.

MUSÉE DU LUXEMBOURG

Map 1; 19 Rue de Vaugirard, 6th; ///moves.tumble.flexed;
www.museeduluxembourg.fr

Often overlooked by out-of-towners, this museum is highly revered by locals – most of whom drop by for a quiet, pre-dinner culture fix on Monday evenings. There are only two exhibitions a year, often on leading figures from the art world, so check ahead and plan your trip well in advance if you have a preference for your art and artists.

CENTRE POMPIDOU

Map 2; Place George Pompidou, 4th; ///ignites.cones.words;
www.centrepompidou.fr

Monday nights at this contemporary art centre belong to a young after-work crowd, all of whom know that when the industrial exterior lights up, the fun is just starting. Every week sees something new grace the calendar, whether it's a monthly film screening or a dance show.

When the Georges closes, head to the nearby cosy bar Le Workshop, open until 2am, for a final glass of wine.

Once the galleries close, those in the know take the escalator up to the rooftop Restaurant Georges, where post-gallery snacks and a view over the city lights continue until midnight.

MUSÉE D'ORSAY

Map 1; 1 Rue de la Légion d'Honneur, 7th; ///pouch.ensemble.flames; www.m.musee-orsay.fr

While this museum is flooded with narrating guides in the day, it's as still as a scene from a Monet painting on Thursday nights, when a sophisticated crowd peter in for evening concerts in the nave or intimate recitals in the auditorium. Instrumental crescendos make a stroll through the Impressionist art galleries all the more romantic.

» Don't leave without getting the perfect shot of Paris from above through the clock face on the fifth floor, with views over the Seine.

CITÉ DE L'ARCHITECTURE ET DU PATRIMOINE

Map 6; 1 Place du Trocadéro et du 11 Novembre, 16th; ///pricier.demand.forgets; www.citedelarchitecture.fr

Parisians are pretty into their architecture – unsurprising given how photogenic the city's buildings are. This spot charts the development of French architecture, and locals know there's no better time to visit than on Thursday nights, when they can end with a fittingly dramatic view of the Eiffel Tower lit up against the dark sky from the upper floors.

PALAIS DE TOKYO

Map 6; 13 Avenue du Président Wilson, 16th; ///connects.chambers.wiser;
www.palaisdetokyo.com

You'll rarely see a painting in the concrete-clad exhibition spaces here.
Instead, there's a heavy focus on multimedia and sensory installations,
and works are often confrontational. A young, free-thinking crowd
ponder the programme at the nightly openings, when a roster of
boundary-pushing concerts, performances and screenings often
come with a party vibe until midnight. The terrace, with great views
across to the Eiffel Tower, is the prime spot to reflect after a show.

MUSÉE DU LOUVRE

Map 1; 91–3 Rue de Rivoli, 1st; ///keyboard.detection.cups; www.louvre.fr

Embark on one evening visit to the Louvre and, like any true Parisian,
you'll never go in the daytime again. While that has a lot to do with
the lack of giggling school groups and selfie-takers, it's also more
atmospheric at night, when a whole other world under the museum

The Louvre may be huge, but
it's hard to find a quiet corner
during the day, and you're likely
to see the *Mona Lisa* only
through someone's smartphone.
Yet it is possible to escape the
crowds within the heart of the
world's most-visited museum:
go upstairs to the Northern
European painters or to the
wings housing Islamic art,
where tourists groups rarely go.

comes alive with concerts and lectures on art history. It's the live music that mostly draws in the post-work crowds, with international chamber music on Wednesday nights and more classic performances on Friday – just turn up by 7pm before the ticket office closes and enjoy.

» **Don't leave without** taking in the night lighting of I M Pei's famous pyramid outside, which seems dull during the day by contrast.

PALAIS GALLIERA

Map 6; 10 Avenue Pierre 1er de Serbie, 16th;
///caked.gangway.remodel; www.palaisgalliera.paris.fr

There's always a buzz in the air when this fashion museum opens its doors. It only stages two exhibitions a year, showcasing part of its 200,000-piece collection of clothing and accessories. As a result, attending an exhibit is an exclusive event, made all the more special on Thursday nights, when it stays open until 9pm. Budding designers and fashion students don their best outfits and trawl the halls of this Beaux-Arts palace, while the sun sets outside the bay windows.

MUSÉE DES ARTS ET MÉTIERS

Map 2; 60 Rue Réamur, 3rd; ///mint.drew.struts; www.arts-et-metiers.net

Not interested in the industrial arts? Think again. This underrated museum tempts end-of-the-week revellers inside with free admission after 6pm on a Friday, and the expansive collection of century-old bicycles and other curious gizmos makes them stay until closing at 9pm. It's set in the remains of an old priory, and the contrast between science and religion is lost on few who wander its halls.

Modern Art

Paris has always led the trends when it comes to art (Monet and Dalí, anyone?), and the city continues to shake up the scene today. Contemporary works make their way into vibrant spaces that rival the Louvre.

GALERIE PERROTIN

Map 2; 76 Rue de Turenne, 3rd; ///havens.cinemas.hill; www.perrotin.com

This international gallery is one for serious modern art fans. It rarely makes its way onto the tourist roster, rather attracting collectors and visitors from Hong Kong and New York (where some of Perrotin's other galleries are to be found). They all come to ponder exhibits by rising artists as well as big names like Takashi Murakami. It may be prestigious, but you won't feel out of place if you're not an art critic.

59 RIVOLI

Map 1; 59 Rue de Rivoli, 1st; ///digress.stewing.belong; www.59rivoli.org

The city's original art squat still feels counter-cultural, its quirky façade wedged amid the shops on commercial Rue de Rivoli. Now a colourful gallery (think art scribbled on each stairwell and stacked canvases teetering in each room) with working studios, 59 Rivoli is an inclusive space where free-thinking artists create away while chatting to the

A new exhibition is held on the ground floor every fortnight, so check the website to see what's on.

artsy Parisians who watch them at work. Come the weekend, revellers pack out every inch of the space for free musical concerts and performances.

LE BAL

Map 4; 6 Impasee de la Défense, 18th;
///blue.reaction.pastime; www.le-bal.fr

This former dance hall turned small non-profit gallery is so acutely Parisian. Exhibitions here use photography, video and new media to focus on "multiple possible approaches to reality", so it gets pretty philosophical, but that's why it's unique. By hosting thought-provoking shows from young artists and regular talks to accompany them, Le Bal dares to do something different, and dares to do it well.

» **Don't leave without** visiting the café, one of the earliest in Paris to serve gourmet brew in a coffee shop setting.

HALLE SAINT-PIERRE

Map 4; 2 Rue Ronsard, 18th; ///sushi.october.cool; www.hallesaintpierre.org

Montmartre may have a touristy reputation when it comes to its art scene, but while out-of-towners browse the canvas-lined stalls in Place du Tertre, avant-garde arty types escape to this cultural centre for an antidote to the mainstream. Inside a former market hall at the foot of the Sacré-Coeur you'll find creatives pouring over unconventional forms of art at their leisure before sharing their views on the exhibitions over an espresso in the café.

ATELIER DES LUMIÈRES

Map 3; 38 Rue Saint-Maur, 11th; ///waitress.finders.newest;
www.atelier-lumieres.com

Missing out on an exhibition at this ground-breaking digital art gallery is such a travesty that Parisians go into a frenzy to nab tickets months in advance. This cultural spot has revitalized the fine art scene and made it accessible to all walks of life – you won't find any light-filled galleries with static portraits here. Instead, your visit is on your terms, whether you want to lie on the floor to watch moving works of art projected onto the ceiling or stand in the centre of a room, transfixed by the colours beneath your feet that move to the beats of music.

FONDATION LOUIS VUITTON

Map 6; 8 Avenue du Mahatma Gandhi, 16th; ///miles.spooked.invent;
www.fondationlouisvuitton.fr

Though this striking building is tucked away in the bucolic Bois de Boulogne, it's no secret, rising above the trees like billowing sails. The space is dedicated to contemporary art (rather than Vuitton's

Try it!
PICK A PASTEL

Inspired to create your own masterpiece? Head to La Maison du Pastel *(www. lamaisondupastel.com)*, the world's oldest pastel manufacturer, to stock up on some tools. It's only open on Thursday afternoons.

signature fashion) and the unconventional exhibitions demand as much attention as the exterior, drawing creatives who religiously trek from the centre of Paris to attend new openings.

» **Don't leave without** seeing the view of Paris's skyline from the rooftop terrace. It's a unique vantage you won't find elsewhere.

MAISON EUROPÉENNE DE LA PHOTOGRAPHIE

Map 2; 5/7 Rue de Fourcy, 4th; ///glue.chairs.fairway; www.mep-fr.org

There's no place for frivolousness at this house of photography. Budding photographers get a close-up look at black-and-white works by notable artists, couples stroll hand in hand past avant-garde portraits in delicate frames and intrigued visitors ponder fine art shots with their heads craned. It's a sacred and minimalist affair, where neutral walls let the photos speak for themselves.

FONDATION CARTIER POUR L'ART CONTEMPORAIN

Map 6; 261 Boulevard Raspail, 14th; ///miss.shelved.various; www.fondationcartier.com

Few private foundations are appreciated by Parisians due to the city's many accessible public collections, but this foundation for contemporary art bucks that trend. Progressive works by artists – many young and relatively unknown – from different backgrounds draw a similar mix of bloggers, trendy locals and inquisitive students, who drop in for the visionary temporary exhibitions.

Esoteric Collections

There are museums, and then there are museums. Paris has a host of quirky and oftentimes hyper-specific collections that will surprise and capture your attention (perhaps more than the **Mona Lisa***).*

MUSÉE DU QUAI BRANLY–JACQUES CHIRAC

Map 6; 37 Quai Branly, 7th; ///outfit.biggest.tonic; www.quaibranly.fr
Behind a distinctive vegetal façade created by the inventor of the vertical garden, Patrick Blanc, lies the least conventional of Paris's big museums. Many of the objects and artworks housed in the modern ethnographic collections – African instruments, Aztec statues and Gabonese masks – were first displayed in 18th-century cabinets of curiosities as treasures "discovered" during colonization in Africa, Asia, Oceania and the Americas. These days, the curation is rather more nuanced and many of the exhibitions are superb, tempting Parisians to flock to every opening. The focus today is on cultural connection and dialogue, but some activists are still calling for the return of artifacts to their original home.

» Don't leave without ambling through the outside grounds, which offer ample breathing and thinking space after touring the museum's collections. In the summer, you might catch a music or dance show.

MUSÉE DES ARTS FORAINS

Map 6; 53 Avenue des Terroirs de France, 12th; ///skips.trip.listings;
www.arts-forains.com

Close your eyes and you can almost smell candyfloss wafting through
the air. Curious kids and kidults alike have a soft spot for this living
museum dedicated to fairground arts, where taking a spin on a
hundred-year-old carousel is enough reason to keep returning. Its
founder, Jean-Paul Favand, began collecting rare items such as
German swings and a Hooghuys organ in the 1970s before realizing
that Paris was missing a space where laughter reigned supreme (in
the midst of all the serious war museums). Actor-guides raise spirits
on requisite tours year-round, but the space truly comes alive at
Christmas, when families flock to enjoy it at their own pace and
watch the likes of magicians and puppeteers perform dreamlike
stories. This is the place you'll be telling friends about once home.

MUSÉE JACQUEMART-ANDRÉ

Map 4; 158 Boulevard Haussmann, 8th; ///piglet.juices.infuses;
www.musee-jacquemart-andre.com

You can almost imagine the lavish parties that were held within
this Parisian mansion as you walk inside. The former private home
is a time capsule filled with *objets d'art* – including oodles of 18th-
century paintings and sculptures – collected from around the world
by art lovers Edouard André and Nélie Jacquemart. It's a rare glimpse
into the life once lived by a wealthy couple, where the grand staircase
and winter garden will leave you looking up real estate costs to see
if your budget could get you something similar in Paris.

MUSÉE DE L'ILLUSION

Map 1; 98 Rue Saint-Denis, 1st; ///stews.tweeted.sounding; www.museedelillusion.fr

If your favourite museums are spaces of quiet contemplation, you might want to give this one a miss. Traditional curatorial rules – as well as the rules of gravity and space – are seemingly turned on their head here. Photo-taking is encouraged as you navigate upside-down rooms, discover the Beuchet Chair's mysterious powers and get dizzy in a "vortex tunnel". Come with friends or for a first date (though save the pints for after – it's psychedelic enough).

MUSÉE EDITH PIAF

Map 3; 5 Rue Crespin du Gast, 11th; ///because.ideas.ports; 01 43 55 52 72

Whether or not you've heard of the famed singer Edith Piaf, this little-known eccentric museum will make you feel like you know her intimately. Created by a lifelong fan, and requiring a phone call to enter, this tiny spot displays an expansive collection of painted

Bet you never thought you'd find a museum dedicated to the simple pinball. You'll need to make an appointment with owner Raphael to visit the secret Paris Pinball Museum (*www.pinball-gallery.com*), but it's worth it. The collector has an impeccable knowledge of the history of pinball machinery and lets you play the vintage games for as long as you like.

portraits, private letters and a huge teddy bear owned by Piaf. It's all set inside an apartment once inhabited by the singer herself, so while you amble around the living room and listen to her records, you can't help but feel like she'll appear in her little black dress.

MUSÉE DE MONTMARTRE
Map 4; 8–14 Rue Cortot, 19th; ///pardon.cookies.error;
www.museedemontmartre.fr

The walls of this former meeting place for artists echo with the voices of Renoir, Utrillo and Toulouse-Lautrec, whose works hang here today. Montmartre was once the heart of bohemian Paris, and nothing typifies that legacy quite like this vestige of the past. Peek at Valadon's studio-apartment, imagine days fuelled by absinthe and finish with a view over the vines of Clos Montmartre that inspired the greats.

MUSÉE DE CLUNY
Map 2; 28 Rue du Sommerard, 5th; ///pizzas.intend.vets;
www.musee-moyenage.fr

A medieval treasure trove, housed in a flamboyant Gothic mansion, built on Roman foundations – how's that for a holistic visit? If the architecture doesn't already impress, inside you can ogle the famed *Lady and the Unicorn* tapestries (said to be the *Mona Lisa* of the Middle Ages) and step down into Roman baths to learn about the city when it was just a little outpost called Lutetia.

» Don't leave without seeing the heads of the sculptures atop Notre Dame that were cut off during the Revolution.

On Stage and Screen

Paris's entertainment scene is driven by the characteristics that define the city: a passion for anti-conformism and a strong intellectual legacy. Kitsch musicals, gripping films and innovative dance await.

CINÉMA EN PLEIN AIR

Map 5; Enter at 211 Avenue Jean Jaurès, 19th;
///vital.urban.sourced; www.lavillette.com

As long as the weather co-operates, the free outdoor screenings in the Parc de la Villette are the summer's biggest events, drawing young Parisians and families who aren't afraid to jostle for a spot on the lawn. Those seeking a touch of luxury rent lawn chairs, but most opt for a blanket on the grass. There's a European charm to it all: everyone cheers when the giant screen begins to inflate, and starts tucking into picnics as soon as the film starts.

CINÉ LE GRAND ACTION

Map 2; 5 Rue des Écoles, 5th; ///prefix.vipers.racks; www.legrandaction.com

The simplicity of the big red seats belie the intricate programming scheduled at this neighbourhood theatre. Despite the rise in popularity of Paris's multiplexes, this cinema continues a legacy of noteworthy retrospectives, ranging from independent films to Oscar-nominated pictures. It's a hub for true cinephiles, who come to debate at the film clubs and take notes at the industry talks on everything from the Cohen brothers to niche Russian films.

ROCKY HORROR AT STUDIO GALANDE

Map 2; 42 Rue Galande, 5th; ///stage.kipper.crab; www.studiogalande.fr

The Rocky Horror Picture Show may be a worldwide phenomenon, but it's been so highly embraced by the French that letting loose at this unique mix of film and live action has become a rite of passage. The longest-running tribute to the cult movie has been bringing fans together since 1978 for a night of bold costumes, scandalous jokes and mayhem inside a tiny arthouse cinema. Parisians aren't outrageous very often, but all inhibitions are left at the door here, so come ready to dance and bring a bag of rice. (And make sure you book ahead.)

LE DIVAN DU MONDE

Map 4; 75 Rue des Martyrs, 18th; ///compounds.backs.modes; www.divandumonde.com

This emblematic club remains under the radar to those who think Montmartre's cabaret scene starts and ends at the Moulin Rouge. Dance fanatics beg to differ, knowing the best show in town is put on by Madame Arthur, the troupe that have been performing cheeky spectacles and musical blind tests here since the 1940s.

» Don't leave without dancing into the early hours, long after your Wednesday or Thursday show has ended.

Solo, Pair, Crowd

Whether you've got a day to yourself or are craving an entertaining night with your mates, there's a show to suit.

FLYING SOLO
Popcorn for one
One of the famous Latin Quarter cinemas, the tiny Le Desperado is the perfect place to cosy up and take in a nostalgic flick by yourself.

IN A PAIR
Broadway for besties
Get tickets to a musical at Théâtre Mogador on Rue de Mogador, which adapts crowd favourites, from *Chicago* to *Grease*, into French. It's a lot of fun.

FOR A CROWD
A screen for titans
Space isn't hard to come by at the sumptuous Grand Rex in the 2nd, also known as Europe's largest cinema theatre. Sit back and watch cinematic masterpieces play out on giant screens.

THÉÂTRE DU CHÂTELET

Map 1; 2 Rue Edouard Colonne, 1st; ///detained.owner.shave;
www.chatelet.com

Anything staged here draws musical theatre lovers like moths to a flame. Fans come to see favourites like *West Side Story* performed in English, and keep returning in the hope of witnessing the next Tony Award winner (*An American in Paris* debuted here in 2014, after all).

LE LOUXOR

Map 4; 170 Boulevard de Magenta, 10th; ///bands.command.slime;
www.cinemalouxor.fr

If the walls of this Egyptian Revival venue could talk, they would share stories of families watching movies in the 1920s and parties held by the gay community in the 1980s. After decades of abandonment, Le Louxor was restored to its cinematic glory in 2013 – much to the joy of those who visit as much for the history as for the global films.

» Don't leave without enjoying an apéritif at the bar on the secret rooftop terrace before a cinema screening.

THÉÂTRE DE LA VILLE DE PARIS

Map 2; 2 Place du Châtelet, 4th; ///tingled.halt.promotes;
www.theatredelaville-paris.com

The contemporary dance performed here is always cutting edge, drawing in creatives of a similar disposition. Sure, the modern auditorium is nothing special, but it's all about the innovative shows that have Parisians engaging in deep debates long after they finish.

City History

Paris is a patchwork of groups and movements, whose history is carved in each arrondissement. Reaffirming local pride, whether it's evoking ancient history or immigrant experiences, is always humbling.

MUSÉE CARNAVALET

Map 2; 16 Rue des Francs Bourgeois, 4th; ///stumble.victory.stray; www.carnavalet.paris.fr

Tucked away in the Marais, this underrated museum is only visited by those who know it's here. Spread across two mansions, the collection traces the city's roots back to Neolithic cultures, through ancient times and all the way to the Napoleonic era. It's an unparalleled look at Parisian history, with toy guillotines and old street signs being a few of the oddities to appreciate.

MUSÉE D'ART ET D'HISTOIRE DU JUDAÏSME

Map 2; 71 Rue du Temple, 3rd; ///jaunts.fixated.games; www.mahj.org

It's fitting that a museum dedicated to Jewish culture and history in France takes up space in the Marais, once the epicentre of the Jewish community. Those seeking to learn about their heritage wander the halls of this elegant mansion to see poignant photos one minute and an entire room dedicated to Hanukkah the next. Though the permanent collection is great, it's the thought-provoking talks and powerful temporary art exhibits that really draw inquisitive minds.

INSTITUT DU MONDE ARABE
Map 2; 1 Rue des Fossés Saint Bernard, 5th;
///crowbar.repair.display; www.imarabe.org

Many locals possess Arabic roots, but Paris was lacking a space that fostered the links between the Arab world and France until this cultural institute opened in the 1980s. Though tourists visit for its architecture – a contemporary build designed around the *mashrabiyya* – the interior draws a mixed crowd. Creatives trawl the Islamic art exhibits, academics bury themselves in tomes in the library and students book on to Arabic language courses.

>> Don't leave without stopping for mint tea on the ninth-floor terrace café, which offers impeccable views over the city.

Shh!

Unbeknown to most locals, underneath Notre Dame lies an unsuspected vestige of ancient Paris – the Crypte Archeologique de l'Île de la Cité *(www.crypte.paris.fr)*. As you descend an unassuming stairwell in the plaza, you'll enter a crypt full of intact remains from over 2,000 years ago, which were found under the cathedral during renovations.

BLACK PARIS WALKS, LE PARIS NOIR

Map 2; Start at Place du Panthéon, 5th; ///also.sings.science;
www.exploreparis.com

When Martinique-born Kévi Donat began to feel unsatisfied with the one-sided narrative told on Paris's walking tours, he set out to reveal the city's unspoken Black history on his own. What started for tourists quickly gained traction with a local crowd, no thanks to Kévi's knack for charismatic storytelling, an interactive way of touring (you won't be privy to a run of dull facts) and an infectious passion as he uncovers the roots of a Pan-African literary movement one minute and the legacy of slavery the next. Kévi's English-speaking walks are available privately, but you can't go wrong with his open tour in collaboration with Explore Paris. If you're interested in the intellectual and artistic side of Paris, take "The Pioneers of the Left Bank" and learn about the figures from the Caribbean, Africa and the USA who transformed this part of the city.

PANTHÉON

Map 2; Place du Panthéon, 5th; ///earliest.fallen.tall;
www.paris-pantheon.fr

Strolling through a mausoleum isn't for everyone, but this secular monument is intrinsic to the story of the French Revolution. Originally built as a church, it was transformed into a place to honour the great and the good of the Revolution era (and distinguished French citizens who came later). There's a mere five women buried here compared to 75 men, but in spite of its male bias, it's a fascinating place where locals come to feel inspired and humbled by their legacy. Intellectuals, politicians and historical figures are enshrined in the crypt below, so

To learn about the lesser-told history of women in Paris, take a walking tour with Women of Paris.

writer Victor Hugo and scientist Marie Curie aren't too far from your feet. If it all starts to feel too morbid, climb up to the dome for a panoramic view over the city.

MUSÉE NATIONALE DE L'HISTOIRE DE L'IMMIGRATION

Map 6; 293 Avenue Daumesnil, 12th; ///limp.unhappy.feelers; www.histoire-immigration.fr

Paris is a melting pot of cultures, and this cultural centre devoted to immigration history lets locals comprehend their own identity and that of their country. The permanent exhibition, which sensitively depicts hardships and hopes, is reason enough to visit. But it's the donation gallery that strikes the most chords, with a resonating collection of personal objects and interview tapes that tell intimate stories.

MUSÉE RODIN

Map 6; 77 Rue de Varenne, 7th; ///humid.snares.tower; www.musee-rodin.fr

You can't think of Paris without appreciating its art history; in fact, you can't even visit the city without passing a museum dedicated to a pioneering artist. Of those museums, the former home and atelier of the founder of modern sculpture, Auguste Rodin, stands out. His legacy is felt in more than just the 300 works on display; it's in the gardens he fell in love with and the studio he sculpted in for nine years.

» Don't leave without seeing *The Thinker*, one of Rodin's most celebrated sculptures, amid the blooming roses in the garden.

Community Projects

Redefining the community centre are cool, urban spots taking up space in old buildings and abandoned stations. Places of refuge, these are somewhere all walks of life come together, and all voices are heard.

104 CENTQUATRE

Map 5; 5 Rue Curial, 19th; ///little.fraction.condiment; www.104.fr

This building may have once been the workplace for the city's undertakers (creepy, right?), but Parisians are breathing new life into it today. Creatives clear their minds with a relaxing Qi Gong class in the morning, budding painters pop in for chats with the artists in residence before taking a painting workshop and teenage dancers use the open spaces to practise their new routines in front of passersby.

LA RECYCLERIE

Map 4; 83 Boulevard Orano, 18th; ///outreach.patting.chief; www.larecyclerie.com

Okay, there are chickens, so you know what you're getting into here. Everything at this former railway station is devoted to an eco-friendly ethos of reuse: an urban farm features a communal vegetable patch, seed swaps encourage community building, a workshop lets people drop off items to be repaired in-house, and if things are too broken to fix, the team find a way to give it new life – and teach you how to do it yourself next time. Zero waste may seem like a fantasy, but here, everyone is at least willing to fantasize.

» Don't leave without having a drink on one of the rickety picnic benches along the Petite Ceinture when the sun's out.

LE SHAKIRAIL
Map 5; 72 Rue Riquet, 18th; ///exposing.feels.bundles;
www.shakirail.curry-vavart.com

You know you've arrived when you reach a seemingly abandoned house fronted by messy chairs and stacks of unidentified objects. No, this isn't a squat – it's a shelter for artistic vagabonds. This welcoming cultural centre is a hive of energy, where locals bond over a series of cool events – a ceramics workshop one day, a film screening the next.

Anyone walking past La Mutinerie (*www.lamutinerie.eu*) may assume it's primarily a bar, but it's so much more. This multi-functional safe space brings the LGBTQ+ community together through regular support evenings, monthly tattoo events, self-defence classes and so much more. Better still, it frequently donates 10–15 per cent of turnover to the LGBTQ+ community. It's a welcoming space that refuses to ignore the oppressions that exist within communities.

Liked by the locals

"Pantin is now a vibrant and diverse neighbourhood, where associations and cultural spaces really support the local community."

SORREL STEWART, EXECUTIVE ASSISTANT
AND PANTIN RESIDENT

LA CITÉ FERTILE

Map 6; 14 Avenue Edouard Vaillant, Pantin; ///second.teamed.lives;
www.citefertile.com

Persuading Parisians to venture into the Pantin suburbs (and adopt a
healthier lifestyle) is this eco-conscious development. It's all about
slowing down at this former railway station, so what will it be: a game
of beach volleyball, a meditation session or a plant-growing workshop?

GROUND CONTROL

Map 6; 81 Rue du Charolais, 12th; ///juniors.calls.bill;
www.groundcontrolparis.com

This popular cultural centre gives off the feel of a mini village, housing
all the requisites needed to practically move in. It's the kind of place
where you can thrift shop in the morning, take a dance class with
a local choreographer in the afternoon, join a debate in the early
evening and finish your day with a bite to eat from the food trucks.
» Don't leave without checking out the Objets Trouvés boutique –
half concept store, half cabinet of curiosities – for a unique gift.

LE HASARD LUDIQUE

Map 4; 128 Avenue de Saint Ouen, 18th; ///drain.starred.choppy;
www.lehasardludique.paris

Tattoo events, pub quizzes and *pétanque* matches are just a taste of
the cool events at this communal hub. Thanks to a crowd-funding
initiative set up by three young Parisians, a matching young clientele
now enjoy a bar and concert hall inside this former train station.

9TH

10TH

RUE LA FAYETTE

Ponder paintings in
MUSÉE GUSTAVE MOREAU

Wander through this symbolist painter's one-time family home, transformed into a museum by Moreau and filled with his artworks.

RUE LA

BLVD HAUSSMANN

RUE MONTMARTRE

2ND

The world's oldest pastel producer, La Maison du Pastel has been making Roché pastels since 1720, and on this site since 1906.

PLACE DE LA CONCORDE

1ST

La Seine

RUE DU LOUVRE

BLVD DE SÉBASTOPOL

3RD

BLVD BEAUMARCHAIS

Become acquainted at
59 RIVOLI

Climb a graffiti-covered spiral staircase to dip in and out of the 30 studios at this art squat. The permanent and transient residents are happy for you to watch them at work.

RUE DE RIVOLI

MARAIS

4TH

PL. DE LA BASTILLE

BOULEVARD ST - GERMAIN

BOULEVARD

6TH

RASPAIL

BOULEVARD ST - MICHEL

Traders have been selling books and prints at the bouquinistes' stalls along the Quai de l'Hôtel de Ville for five centuries.

La Seine

MONTPARNASSE

BOULEVARD MONTPARNASSE

5TH

BOULEVARD DE L'HÔPITAL

14TH

BOULEVARD DE PORT-ROYAL

13TH

| 0 metres | 800 |
| 0 yards | 800 |

**Get immersed at
ATELIER DES
LUMIÈRES**

Book a timed "showing"
and experience classical
paintings like never
before: animated and
set to music.

4

AVENUE PARMENTIER

11TH

R. FAIDHERBE

AVENUE DAUMESNIL

12TH

RUE CHALIGNY

BERCY

3

**Lunch at
GROUND
CONTROL**

Swing by this community
-space-meets-food-court
for some treats and to see
if a craft workshop is on.

An afternoon exploring
Paris's art scene

Art takes many forms in Paris. Centuries-old masterpieces adorn the city's world-class museums, while counter-cultural movements make way for new, fresh talents – and all types of art are met with the same level of awe and admiration. This is a city where street art secretly appears overnight, galleries show traditional works in untraditional ways and single-artist museums shed light on the personality as well as artistry of great masters. Parisians love nothing more than to span styles and eras, and debate the intricacies of each, on a lazy afternoon.

1. Musée Gustave Moreau
14 Rue de la Rochefoucauld,
9th; www.musee-moreau.fr
///twisty.crystal.rubble

2. 59 Rivoli
59 Rue de Rivoli, 1st;
www.59rivoli.org
///digress.stewing.belong

3. Ground Control
81 Rue du Charolais,
12th; www.ground
controlparis.com
///juniors.calls.bill

4. Atelier des Lumières
38 Rue Saint-Maur, 11th;
www.atelier-lumieres.com
///waitress.finders.newest

La Maison du Pastel ///tractor.even.palace

Quai de l'Hôtel de Ville ///compiled.sides.swinging

NIGHTLIFE

*Paris's easy-going nature extends
to its nightlife scene. Friends catch
up over apéritifs, groups dance
along the banks of the canal and
musicians play in intimate venues.*

Guinguettes and Rooftops

Drinking outdoors is a Parisian pastime, and one that gets all the more ritualistic on balmy summer nights. As soon as night falls, locals battle for spots on rooftops and at open-air café-bars.

LE PERCHOIR MÉNILMONTANT

Map 3; 14 Rue Crespin du Gast, 11th; ///browser.relate.loaf; www.leperchoir.fr

The Perchoir group may expand their terrace empire each year, but if you hear talk of a "Le Perchoir" in passing, this is the one. It's the place to see and be seen, where trendy locals come to pose on low bed-style benches, rate everyone's best summer outfits and sip cocktails while overlooking the city's rooftops as the sun goes down.

ROSA BONHEUR

Map 5; Parc des Buttes-Chaumont, 2 Avenue de la Cascade, 19th; ///nuzzled.toggle.healers; www.rosabonheur.fr

Tucked inside Parc des Buttes-Chaumont's easternmost entrance, this idyllic *guinguette* (open-air café/bar) is a summer "it" spot. On Sundays, it turns into an unofficial LGBT+ bar (the eponymous

Get to Rosa Bonheur really early – like 3pm early – on Sundays to avoid having to wait in the famously long queues.

realist painter Rosa Bonheur was a lesbian, after all, so it all seems to track). Expect romance blossoming over bottles of rosé (they pretty much dot every table) and a dance to a pop tune or two.

PÉNICHE MARCOUNET

Map 2; Port des Célestins, Quai de l'Hôtel de Ville, 4th;
///proud.dangerously.divided; www.peniche-marcounet.fr

Forget about those Paris movie clichés for a moment: you really can dance to jazz on the banks of the Seine. Instead of couples in 1920s-style frocks and penguin suits, though, picture easy-going crowds perched at wooden pallet tables, drinking beers and sharing plates of BBQ grub while swaying to sultry tunes. That's the exact scene you'll get when you come to this barge bar between May and October.

MAMA SHELTER EAST

Map 6; 109 Rue de Bagnolet, 20th; ///volunteered.riches.snoring;
www.mamashelter.com

It's locals rather than hotel guests who take over this semi-secret rooftop on sunny nights. Hours pass in minutes beneath candy-coloured parasols, with the help of regular rosé top-ups and a pizza or two brought up from the ground-floor pizzeria. The views aren't the best in town, but you'll be having too much fun to notice.

» Don't leave without challenging a stranger to a game of table football (or *baby-foot*) to reveal your competitive side.

Solo, Pair, Crowd

Nothing captures the romance of Paris like gazing out over the city's rooftops with a cocktail in hand.

FLYING SOLO
Artistic tendencies
After checking out the latest exhibition at the Centre Pompidou *(p112)*, splurge on a glass of champagne at Le Georges, the centre's striking rooftop bar-restaurant.

IN A PAIR
Get high
The views from the Terrass' Hotel's rooftop bar will stop you in your tracks: you can see almost the entire city spread out around the Eiffel Tower from this Montmartre hotel. It's the perfect backdrop for a catch-up.

FOR A CROWD
Time to dine
Book a large table at the rooftop bar Brasserie Auteuil in the 16th for pizza and limoncello spritzes, surrounded by a lush green jungle of towering plants.

PAVILLON PUEBLA

Map 5; Parc des Buttes-Chaumont, 39 Avenue Simon Bolivar, 19th;
///milder.juggler.wicked; www.leperchoir.fr

A patio doubles as a cocktail bar with a dance floor at this fairy-light-lit cabin, nestled in the southernmost tip of Parc des Buttes-Chaumont. It feels like the park's communal living space, with mismatched seating scattered around as if the owner just realized friends were arriving, and a pop playlist getting a house party vibe going.

LE TOP DU POINT EPHÉMÈRE

Map 5; 200 Quai de Valmy, 10th; ///bunny.enforced.remover;
www.pointephemere.org

When locals pass this bar and concert venue in the summer, they're on the lookout for one thing: a green flag hanging outside, signalling the opening of the trendy rooftop terrace. It's a laidback spot where a fun young crowd linger for hours on beach chairs, watching the sun set over the Canal Saint-Martin while sipping on a beer.

» Don't leave without checking the venue's schedule while you're here. You might be able to catch drag bingo or a vintage market inside.

LA JAVELLE

Map 6; Port de Javel Bas, 15th; ///shout.pricing.sleep; www.lajavelle.com

The western side of the quay lacked a little something before this modern summer *guinguette* settled here. The view isn't postcard-worthy, but families come for the village fair vibe and friendly atmosphere, catching up while kids play late into the evening.

Music Nights

Banish any preconceived ideas of a pretentious music scene in the French capital. Sure, live jazz has its place, but vinyl-only DJ sets and underground metal gigs tempt Parisians to dance until the early hours.

LA SEINE MUSICALE

Map 6; Île Seguin, 19th; ///minds.decide.eyebrows;
www.laseinemusicale.com

It takes a strikingly modern concert hall of this calibre to persuade the busiest of Parisians to venture to a small island in the Seine. An approach to making orchestral music accessible to all walks of life attracts more than the average opera crowd here, where even non-ticket-holders can appreciate the fantastic acoustics and choir performances going on inside from the big screen outside the venue.

LA BELLEVILLOISE

Map 5; 19–21 Rue Boyer, 20th; ///dressy.gateway.cherry;
www.labellevilloise.com

Only in Paris can a venue span an exhibition space, cultural hub and club with ease. This spot is always a safe bet for a memorable night out, whether you're settling in on a Chesterfield couch to listen

Book a table for the famed Sunday jazz brunch. It's great for large groups, with heaps of good food.

to a live acoustic set after work or letting loose to a DJ spinning Latin American cumbia rhythms and hip-hop tunes on Friday and Saturday nights.

LE MAZETTE

Map 6; 69 Port de la Rapée, 12th; ///extremes.speared.luring; 01 43 45 67 67
Taking over the mooring once held by the legendary floating club Concrete, this barge venue has brought a lighter vibe to the *quais*. Teetering on the edge of both bar and club, it attracts a mixed crowd who party to varied line-ups on three sprawling floors. With disco DJ sets and stand-up-and-sing-with-the-band karaoke, you'll find yourself returning several nights in a row along with the locals.
» Don't leave without checking out the photogenic rooftop deck, complete with strings of fairy lights and its own bar.

SUPERSONIC

Map 3; 9 Rue Biscornet, 12th; ///hatter.sting.slide; www.supersonic-club.fr
The rock and indie scene is very much alive and well at this industrial, multi-floor club. Any tune with a guitar solo goes down well with the hyperactive crowd, who get more raucous as the night wears on – so you can expect a splash of beer or two from a bopping neighbour while the floor vibrates with music. Some big names cross the threshold, but Supersonic also keep things grounded with themed genre nights. Many of the gigs are free before 11pm, but you'll need plenty of stamina to stay till close (6am) like the rest of them.

LA GARE

Map 5; 1 Avenue Corentin Cariou, 19th; ///residual.cooks.ripe

In-the-know crowds trek quietly to the outer edges of the 19th for free jazz gigs and electro nights here, where word-of-mouth draws in the cool kids in the absence of a website and landline. This standing-room-only and graffiti-scrawled venue – once a train station – may be a laidback spot with cheap beers, but absolute silence and respect is enforced for the artists. Between sets, everyone pours out onto the forecourt to chat and smoke before being shh-d as they cram back in.

L'ENTRÉE DES ARTISTES

Map 4; 30 Rue Victor Massé, 9th; ///pancakes.goals.gangway;
www.lentreedesartistespigalle.com

Like many of the best Parisian music venues, this one is hard to define: it's a restaurant, a cocktail bar and a chilled (mostly) jazz club in one. But come Friday and Saturday evening, things start to liven

Shh!

If you want to catch live music out and about in Paris, look for your nearest Kiosque à Musique. These open-air community bandstands dot parks and squares across Paris and are open to both amateurs and pros. For information on what's coming up, check out www.paris.fr/kiosques, or leave it up to chance and stroll the city: those in Parc Montsouris and Jardin Nelson Mandela are among the most accessible.

up with vinyl-only DJ sets that attract a chic crowd. Tunes might span jazz, gospel, disco or soul – usually with a strong Brazilian or African beat – but whatever's playing, the party keeps going until 5am. It's the place to be in Pigalle at the weekend.

ÉGLISE ST SULPICE

Map 1; 2 Rue Palatin, 6th; ///unhappy.guard.boater; www.classictic.com
Paris's churches all start to blend together, but an organ recital or concert at this nearly regal church – the city's second-largest house of worship – will be memorable. It's a rite of passage for families to attend holiday concerts here, but you don't need to wait until Christmas to hear the pipes do their thing. Simply book ahead for one of the classical evening concerts and settle into the church pews; the impressive acoustics and stained-glass windows make for a spellbinding treat (a glass of wine is optional, but suggested).

PHILHARMONIE DE PARIS

Map 5; 221 Avenue Jean Jaurès, 19th; ///qualified.chilling.creeps;
www.philharmoniedeparis.fr
Don't spend too long debating the controversial, glitzy spaceship-like exterior of this concert hall: it's all about the music and the modern acoustic technology once you're inside. The futuristic theatre itself features innovative seating, so there's no bad spot in the house from which to enjoy a bit of live jazz or a symphony performance.
» Don't leave without checking out the museum, which tends to host special exhibits dedicated to musical figures and greats.

Game Night

*Gaming culture flies under the radar in Paris, but it's surprisingly strong. Whether you have a penchant for board games or fancy trying your hand at **pétanque**, there's always a playground for the young at heart.*

CHEZ BOUBOULE

Map 3; 26 Avenue Jean Aicard, 11th; ///faster.players.share; www.chezbouboule.fr

One of three spots to share the same name and concept, this indoor *pétanque* bar is party central at the weekend, when you can hardly see or hear the matches in action over the chatter and music. Bring a group of friends, get here early and chalk your names on the wall to secure a slot on the pitch. You don't need your own set of balls, but

Try it!
PLAY PÉTANQUE

Once you've mastered the French art of *pétanque*, take it outdoors. Games on the terrains backing the Quai de la Loire *(p152)* tend to be relaxed, while more serious matches go on late along Rue Botzaris.

you will need a grasp of the rules: getting your boules as close as possible to the jack. Knocking your opponents out of the way is encouraged, as is sipping on a Lillet and tonic as you strategize.

RESET

Map 1; 17 Rue du Cygne, 1st; ///deserved.handbag.scout; www.reset.bar
Stroll a few minutes through the bar-filled backstreets north of Châtelet and you'll stumble across this time machine, ready to transport you back to childhood. At this bar-meets-video-game paradise, a raft of classic arcade and console games have been brought back to life. The screens are the décor here, and Atari, Street Fighter II and early Nintendo 64 smash-hits like Goldeneye 007 are just the start of the retro mania. Everyone from square-eyed gamers to daters in search of a nostalgic night out come to find their own slice of fun.

» Don't leave without ordering a sweet and creamy Bomberman cocktail with rum, amaretto, cream, vanilla and cinnamon. Think of it as a (grown-up) throwback to a milkshake.

LE BAR À PINTES

Map 3; 111 Rue Saint-Maur, 11th; ///letter.shins.stewing; www.lebap.fr
Proper dive bars are hard to come by in Paris, and bars with pool tables even more so, which makes this sometimes rowdy spot, signed as "Le BAP" from the street, worth seeking out. It's opted for a French spin on Americana, so expect references to *baby-foot* and billiards rather than foosball and pool. The generous happy hour prices will give you the confidence to challenge strangers to a game or two.

GAMELLE

**Map 3; 29 Avenue Daumesnil, 12th; ///protest.salutes.refrain;
www.gamelle-paris.fr**

You'd be forgiven for thinking Gamelle is just a regular bar from the
crowds drinking outside. But elbow your way through and you'll enter
a loft-style hangout, where a mini bowling lane, pinball tables and a
dart board await you and your most competitive friends. Sipping on
a Gin To' Gamelle — Gamelle's signature gin and tonic with fresh
mint and cinnamon — is pretty mandatory between turns.

GOSSIMA PING PONG BAR

Map 3; 4 Rue Victor Gelez, 11th; ///homing.agreeing.verse; www.gossima.fr

Ping pong and pints make for the perfect combination at this bar,
where nights are set to the echo of balls flying on and off the tables
(and occasionally the walls). Good tunes and great cheese boards
make this a popular party venue, but plenty of friends also stop by for
a little one-on-one competition still suited from the office early in the
evening. Eight tables are spread across two sparsely decorated
floors and a private room, so book ahead to get a table.

À LA FOLIE PARIS

**Map 5; Parc de la Villette, 19th; ///ramming.correct.pylons;
www.alafolie.paris**

It's all fun and games at this self-styled *néo-guinguette* out in the Parc
de La Villette, one of the few parks where only Parisians tend to tread.
It's a bit of an indoor-outdoor playground that welcomes anyone up

for a good time. In summer, that means rounds of Mölkky (Finnish skittles) between sips of drinks at picnic tables; in winter, expect raucous games of drag bingo (one of few drag events in Paris) indoors.

LE DERNIER BAR AVANT LA FIN DU MONDE

Map 1; 19 Avenue Victoria, 1st; ///obeyed.juices.lodge; www.lastbar.com
You'll roam from steampunk to Star Destroyer on the different levels of this geek enclave, where devoted Parisians huddle over board games with a drink for company. Grab a beer, choose from the vast selection of games – in all states of pre-loved distress – and settle in. It's a haven for sci-fi fans, so you might want to prepare a *Star Wars* or *Lord of the Rings* reference to impress the regulars (though if you're heading here already, you probably don't need coaching).
» Don't leave without grabbing a refreshing C3PO fruit mocktail infused with vanilla. You need your wits to win, right?

BOWLING DE PARIS FRONT DE SEINE

Map 6; 15 Rue Gaston de Caillavet; ///puddles.uptake.speak; www.xbowlingsympas.com
Sure, Parisians are more known for schooling opponents over a game of *pétanque* than a round of bowling, but these lanes, connected to a swanky shopping mall, teem with locals nonetheless. Drumming up memories of birthday parties and first dates, this beloved hall draws groups of friends and families with kids in tow every night of the week looking for an excuse to let loose after work and school.

Open-air Living Rooms

When the sun goes in, Parisians refuse to do the same. Every inch of the city's streets become communal backyards after dark, with locals gathering to drink, socialize and dance outdoors.

QUAI DE LA LOIRE

Map 5; Quai de la Loire, 19th; ///husbands.pinch.gifts

This broad, calm canal is a local alternative to the Seine – and with more action. Parisians use its wide banks for *pétanque* matches, which start late in the day and continue into the evening. Bring your own set and stake out a spot; if you haven't packed these heavy metal balls, the nearby BarOurcq usually rents out sets for those lucky enough to get there before they're gone.

CANAL SAINT-MARTIN

Map 5; Canal Saint-Martin, 10th; ///towns.requested.ketchup

The din of evening revellers can be heard up the street as you approach this hotspot. Students and edgy locals mingle late into the night here, cradling a few beers and tucking into hummus from the

Order a pizza at Pink Flamingo and you'll be given a bright balloon as a "ticket" – simply find a spot on the quay and wait. local grocery store as they occupy every last centimetre of space along the canal. On the hottest summer evenings, the most daring of the groups jump from the arching iron bridges to cool off.

PONT MARIE

Map 2; Pont Marie, 4th; ///shows.compose.stubborn

The 17th-century *pont* (bridge) itself is unremarkable, but this bend in the Rives de Seine park is a popular gathering spot for evening picnics, where wine corks pop and crusty baguettes break. Find a free bit of cobblestone along the riverbanks, dangle your legs above the water and await the best sunsets over the Seine. There are floating bars and cafés along the water if you run out of food and drink supplies (or simply if the wind sets in).

PLACE DU MARCHÉ SAINTE-CATHERINE

Map 2; Place du Marché Sainte-Catherine, 4th; ///crew.mutual.uptake

While out-of-towners overlook this little leafy square in favour of nearby Place des Vosges, locals take advantage of the space here, chatting on the benches over a pitcher of wine from one of the cafés that line the plaza. It becomes one big communal terrace at night, when impromptu musicians fill the air with lively tunes and the laughter and conversation carry on till late.

» Don't leave without getting a glass of rosé from Chez Joséphine around the square's edge to enjoy while the sun sets.

PONT DES ARTS

Map 1; Pont des Arts, 6th; ///grades.wipes.airless

This bridge practically doubles as a giant couch. Lovers gazing at
the sunset, an artist painting a landscape on an easel, a busker
strumming a song – those Paris clichés are all here. The romantic
edge dates back to the time when clunky rusty metal padlocks gave
this bridge the nickname "love lock bridge"; though the locks have
gone, it's still a charming place to bring a bottle of bubbly, take a
seat against the railings and sip the night away.

JARDIN TINO-ROSSI

Map 2; 2 Quai Saint-Bernard, 5th; ///vitals.trams.sleep

There's nothing dreamier than dancing on the banks of the Seine on
a balmy Parisian night. During the summer, cha-cha, hip-hop and
ballet sessions are a regular sight in the small amphitheatres along
this riverside park, but it's the tango dancing that draws most locals.

Tango dancing on the Seine
may be a popular event in the
summer, but those that dread
coming unprepared head
to the riverbank at 7pm – an
hour and a half before the
performances start – for
a free tango lesson. They're held
by Tango Argentin, the friendly
organizers of the dancing
event at Jardin Tino-Rossi, from
Wednesday to Sunday, June
through September. Simply turn
up with a pair of comfy shoes.

Ladies bring their dancing shoes, skirts catch in the breeze and things heat up until midnight. Don't have a partner? Someone will pick you out of the crowd, so prepare to swing and dip (or gracefully decline from the sidelines). Audrey Hepburn would totally approve.

» Don't leave without exploring the Musée de la Sculpture en Plein Air, where you'll find sculptures by the likes of Ossip Zadkine.

JARDIN DU CARROUSEL
Map 1; Place du Carrousel, 1st; ///fest.slacker.sifts

The grassy gardens directly in front of the Louvre are far from a secret, but unknown to out-of-towners is the fact that they're open all night. Friends come for post-work wind-downs, stretching out with a blanket and nibbling on a baguette while the odd frisbee gets their attention flying overhead. It doesn't get more Parisian than seeing the Eiffel Tower illuminated in the distance and the palatial museum sitting behind you.

JARDIN NELSON MANDELA
Map 1; 1 Place du René Cassin, 1st; ///dude.beefed.rust

When you spot the giant statue of a head, you've arrived. Known to locals as Jardin Les Halles, the area in the shadows of St Eustache church has had a facelift in recent years, with heaps of seating added that make it more amenable to hanging out than ever before. By day, parents watch their kids in the playground, but by night, the green space becomes the domain for friends catching up before heading off to the nearby Marais.

Apéritif Spots

A quick pre-dinner apéritif (or **apéro***) is a sacred tradition in Paris, marking the transition from day to night. When work days end, it's straight to a bar where fuss and reservations are not on the menu.*

AGROLOGY

Map 3; 15 Rue de Prague, 12th; ///rails.homework.december; 01 58 51 05 49

At a glance you could easily mistake Agrology for a wine shop and grocery store, but there's just enough space for a few start-of-evening drinks – either inside or on a pavement table in good weather. The bottle selection has a Mediterranean leaning, with plenty of wines from beyond France's borders: a welcome change when many *apéro* hours mean a choice between Beaujolais, Bordeaux and Chablis.

LE LABO

Map 1; 37 Rue des Lombards, 1st; ///surviving.frantic.bounty; www.thelabo.fr

There's always high energy at this LGBT+ haven, where students, couples and trendy folk spill out onto the pavement terrace with cheap drinks to get riled up for the rest of the night. There are lots of gay bars in the area, but Le Labo is notably larger and more welcoming to all genders, sexes and sexualities, so is the spot of choice for those seeking a quick drink in a friendly atmosphere. Pop in for a happy hour beer on Tuesday, when drinks are even cheaper, the crowd even rowdier and intimate conversations a no-go.

CAFÉ DU COIN

Map 3; 9 Rue Camille Desmoulins, 11th; ///fellow.inserted.blaring; 01 48 04 82 46

When you find a café that opens at 8am for locals to drink espresso bleary-eyed at the bar, then stays busy all the way through to 2am most nights a week, you know you're onto a good thing. Though the affordable lunchtime *formules* draw office workers weekly, it's the always heaving *apéro* that people tell their colleagues about. Meet your friends early to sate your pre-dinner hunger with a pizzette and a glass of natural wine to see what all the fuss is about.

» **Don't leave without** trying the seemingly simplest (but tastiest) pizzette of the day, usually topped with mozzarella, ham and harissa.

PIGNON

Map 4; 9 Rue Brochant, 17th; ///senses.apron.publish

It's easy to see why the 17th is increasingly being hailed one of the city's coolest quartiers when you stop for a drink at Pignon. It's the kind of place where friends meet after work to sip on bottles of Parisian-brewed beer, tuck into sharing plates and shout over a few games of table football before wandering onwards in search of dinner. In short: a casual spot to get a taste of the Batignolles bar scene.

LE PETIT FER Á CHEVAL

Map 2; 30 Rue Vieille du Temple, 4th; ///bridge.waffle.horses;
www.cafeine.com/petit-fer-a-cheval

This traditional café-bistro is one of renowned Marais restaurateur's Xavier Denamur's clutch of addresses, so it's a bit of an institution. It's a tiny spot, and the pavement tables are too small to comfortably settle into for long, but this makes it the perfect place to drop by for a quick glass of rosé before moving on.

CRAVAN

Map 6; 17 Rue Jean de la Fontaine, 16th; ///fend.verse.defended

The sleepy 16th was once the last place you'd go for a well-made drink, but thanks to Cravan, it's finally shaking off its reputation as a cocktail desert. Strong drinks served in elegant coupe glasses are the speciality here, so even one will get your night off to a storming start.

» Don't leave without trying The Tunnel, a sophisticated twist on a Negroni, with Noilly Prat, Campari and Punt E Mes, served straight.

LA FONTAINE

Map 5; 31–3 Rue Juliette Dodu, 10th; ///migrants.bucket.cobbles;
www.cafesbelleville.com

Once easily overlooked, this quintessential corner café is now reimagined in all but appearance. Set up a few blocks from the canal, it draws more locals and devotees than tourists for the creative cocktails and nibbles – great for a quick stop on your way to dinner or more drinks along the canal.

Liked by the locals

"*Apéro* is another reason to make eating and drinking last all night, rather than a few hours. It's an early happy hour with finger food and friends that gets you ready for a big meal."

BARBARA DONADELLO, EVENTS PLANNER

2ND

RUE ÉTIENNE MARCEL

RUE DE TURBIGO

**Get a culture fix at
MUSÉE DU LOUVRE**
Wander the halls before
close (6pm, unless it's a late
opening), and admire the
pyramid at golden hour.

3RD

Since 2019, the
renowned theatre and
opera house **Théâtre
du Châtelet** has been
home to hidden night
club, Club Joséphine.

1 1ST

QUAI F. MITTERAND

La Seine

QUAI DE LA
MEGISSERIE

Q. DE GESVRES

PLACE
DE L'HÔTEL
DE VILLE

MARAIS

RUE DE RIVOLI

4TH

2

Île de
la Cité

3 Q. DE CELESTINS

**Bag a spot at
SQUARE DU
VERT-GALANT**
Dangle your feet above
the Seine at the western
end of Île de la Cité,
sharing an *apéro* while
the city lights sparkle.

LATIN
QUARTER

BLVD ST - GERMAIN

**Sway to music at
PÉNICHE
MARCOUNET**
Catch a live jazz show on the
atmospheric terrace of this
péniche (barge) while tucking
into sharing plates of food.

Île St-
Louis

QUAI HENRY IV

La Seine

6TH

BOULEVARD ST - MICHEL

RUE ST - JACQUES

5TH

RUE MONGE

QUAI ST - BERNARD

13TH

BOULEVARD DE L'HÔPITAL

| 0 metres | 500 |
| 0 yards | 500 |

An evening following
the Seine path

The Seine is as much at the heart of Paris after dark as it is during the day. On sunny evenings, it's Parisians, not visitors, that pack the *quais* to watch the sunset over the water. Nights out start late and continue at a relaxed pace, so you can catch an exhibition, stroll along the river, have an apéritif or two and only start to think about where you might dance the night away around 11pm. Parisians aren't generally big plan-makers when it comes to bar-hopping: just follow the river's calling and see where the evening takes you.

1. Musée du Louvre
91–3 Rue de Rivoli, 1st;
www.louvre.fr
///keyboard.detection.cups

2. Square du Vert-Galant
15 Place du Pont Neuf, 1st
///results.faces.examples

3. Péniche Marcounet
Port des Célestins, Quai de l'Hôtel de Ville, 4th;
www.peniche-marcounet.fr
///proud.dangerously.divided

4. Le Mazette
69 Port de la Rapée, 12th;
01 43 45 67 67
///extremes.speared.luring

Théâtre du Châtelet ///detained.owner.shave

**Dance at
LE MAZETTE**
Head east when things get quieter in central Paris after 12am. This huge bar-boat has DJ sets until 2am most days.

OUTDOORS

Outdoor living is essential to Paris, where apartments are notoriously compact. Manicured parks, cobbled plazas and scenic riversides afford the space and freedom locals relish.

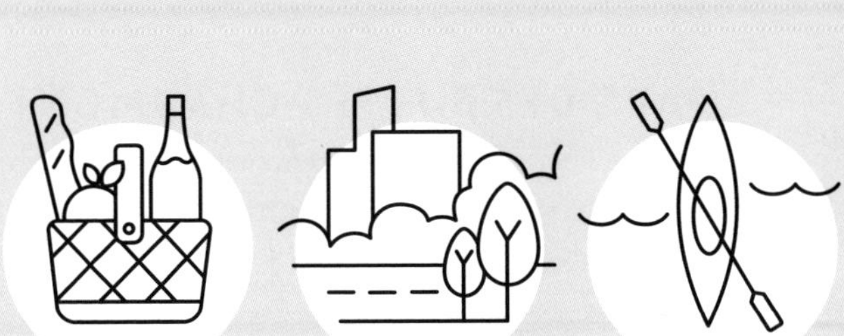

Picnic Spots

As soon as the sun peeks through the clouds, locals grab a blanket and flock to grassy lawns. Picnics embody what Paris is all about: a relaxed pace of life, picturesque settings, great food and perfect company.

JARDIN DU PALAIS ROYAL

Map 1; enter at 9 Rue de Beaujolais, 1st; ///fluid.outgoing.bind; www.domaine-palais-royal.fr

Often overlooked by the crowds who pack into the nearby Louvre, this tree-lined garden offers some unexpected peace and quiet in the 1st. At lunchtime, workers come here to take it easy, lining the benches and tucking into mini picnics of pastries and takeaway coffees. Pull up one of the metal chairs scattered by the central fountain with a book and relax.

PARC DES BUTTES-CHAUMONT

Map 5; enter at Rue Manin and Avenue Secrétan, 19th; ///diverts.revision.asserts; 01 48 03 83 10

Hot summer weekends are abuzz with locals of all dispositions packing out this enormous hilltop park. Sun-worshippers while away a whole day here, strolling around the small lake, relaxing with a glass of wine and watching the sun set from the little temple at the top. The park's features are all part of the 19th-century redesign of Paris, but no one balks at the artifice. It feels natural, and that's why it's a firm favourite for picnic gatherings.

PARC MONCEAU
Map 4; enter at Place de la République Dominicaine, 8th;
///gasp.attend.warnings

The only thing posher than the elegant apartments in the 8th arrondissement is this tiny bijou park, where well-heeled groups of girlfriends organize their sophisticated picnics. Decorative ruins and cherry blossom in the spring create an idyllic backdrop for breaking bread on the grass and snapping a photo beside wicker picnic baskets. You may hesitate to leave any crumbs (these are Paris's most genteel grounds, after all), but what's a picnic without them?
» Don't leave without picking up fresh picnic supplies from the nearby Marché des Batignolles if you're visiting on a Saturday.

You won't just stumble upon Jardin Anne Frank *(14P Impasse Berthaud, 3rd)*, a tiny oasis tucked away in the Marais. Surrounded by apartment buildings, it feels like a lost urban playground, manicured but simultaneously a little wild. It pays homage to Anne Frank, making it a tranquil spot to come and contemplate while eating a pastry on a bench.

JARDIN DU LUXEMBOURG
Map 1; enter at Rue de Vaugirard, 6th; ///deputy.bouncing.talking;
01 42 34 20 00

While families settle on the metal chairs that surround the fountains, youngsters head to the grassy knolls at the south of the park – the only green patch where lounging is permitted. On summer days, this southern boundary is invaded by students toasting the end of exams and friends celebrating birthdays, all of them armed with a bottle of wine and fresh supplies from nearby Marché St-Germain.

PARC DE BERCY
Map 6; 128 Quai de Bercy, 12th; ///studio.because.piles

There's a relaxed residential character to these contemporary gardens, where those who live nearby come for a post-work catch up on balmy nights. Located next to the old wine warehouses of Bercy Village, it's a convenient area to pick up a bottle or two before settling on the lawns. There are reliable public restrooms available, too, which means you can broach that extra bottle of wine worry-free.

Try it!
GET GARDENING

If spending all that time in pretty parks has got your green fingers itching, check out a gardening workshop at Maison du Jardinage (www.jardinons-ensemble.org), an information centre in Parc de Bercy.

PLACE DES VOSGES

Map 2; Place des Vosges, 4th; ///ankle.terms.planting

If the sun's out, expect to fight for a space on the very grounds where royals once jousted (though you'll be armed with baguettes rather than swords). Like the neighbourhood in which it resides, this pretty square attracts an assortment of people: out-of-towners lounging in the sun, children playing in the sand, joggers huffing around the perimeter. There's no better place for a people-watching picnic.

BOIS DE VINCENNES

Map 6; enter at Avenue François Fresneau, 12th;
///casually.foiled.reheat; 01 49 57 15 15

When school's out for summer, families pack the sandwiches and head to this huge country escape. Part of the fun of picnicking here is wandering the paths for a secluded spot on the shoreline – an idyllic spot from which to watch boaters pass. Exploring the adjoining arboretum and château after the picnic is mandatory.

» Don't leave without renting a rowboat along the Lac Daumesnil to discover two tiny islands and a picturesque little gazebo.

PLACE LOUIS ARAGON

Map 2; Place Louis Aragon, Île Saint-Louis, 4th; ///locker.ticking.yappy

Sitting at the tip of Île Saint-Louis, this cutesy cobbled terrace is the sunset-watching spot of choice for date nights. Couples cosy up, dangling their legs just a few metres from the Seine below, while boats float by, buskers strum guitars and wine corks pop. Divine.

Urban Adventures

Sure, Parisians have a knack for enjoying a leisurely pace of life, but it's all about balance. The city is an urban playground that tempts everyone to get active and explore (even if only to indulge in a coffee after).

CYCLE THE CANAL

Map 3; start at Port de l'Arsenal, 4th; ///indeed.ember.grudges; www.velib-metropole.fr

Rolling through the city, the breeze in your face as you lazily ride along the river for what seems like hours, is about as local as it gets. But skip the well-trodden Seine trails. Rent a Vélib bike and cycle along the canal from the picturesque Port de l'Arsenal, past picnickers to the green expanse of Parc de la Villette. Don't forget to pack a baguette in your basket to look *really* Parisian.

JOG THE BOIS DE BOULOGNE

Map 6; Porte Dauphine, 16th; ///trading.infects.hoping; 01 53 92 82 82

As soon as the sun rises, athletic Parisians head to this beloved patch of greenery, which has become something of a runner's paradise in a city not known for tolerating joggers. For the non-early risers, the paths and trails become afternoon escapes, where

Come back at night for La Clairière, an enchanting place with a club atmosphere, to party to great music.

getting lost among wooded areas and waterfronts or admiring the park's centuries-old architecture is the perfect accompaniment to a calming playlist.

RIDE THE BALLON DE PARIS GENERALI

Map 6; Parc André-Citroën, 15th; ///charging.inched.workshops; www.ballondeparis.com

Once an activity reserved for the upper classes, hot-air ballooning is now open to everyone – and locals are all for it. Seeing the world's largest tethered balloon in the skyline is impressive enough, but viewing the city from an altitude of 150 m (500 ft) from the balloon itself is unparalleled (just ensure it's a fine day, as wind tends to ground it). It's also a tool for raising awareness of air pollution, with blinking lights indicating air quality, so you get a bit of an education, too.

STROLL THE COULÉE VERTE

Map 3; 1 Coulée Verte René-Dumon, 12th; ///dealings.held.water

The inspiration for NYC's highline (despite what New Yorkers might tell you) runs along an old viaduct from Bastille to the Bois de Vincennes. Although some sections dip to ground level, the majority offers a nice elevated hike through the city. It's pretty narrow, so Parisians on their work breaks know not to stop and linger lest they cause a traffic jam, reserving such follies for *les touristes*. You've been warned.

» Don't leave without checking out the artsy shops under the arches at the beginning of the walking route.

JOG THE PARC RIVES DE SEINE

Map 3; start at 2–4 Quai Henri IV, 4th; ///homework.scooter.years

If you hit the pedestrianized Right or Left Banks at the same time each day, you'll begin to spot the same joggers in their trainers and tanks. Paris's runners were thrilled when this park opened in 2017, allowing them to log miles without pesky traffic lights stopping their flow. It follows the path of the Paris Marathon: start by Bastille, run towards the Louvre, cross over to the Left Bank by the Musée d'Orsay and head towards the Eiffel Tower for a workout with a view.

FIND THE PETITE CEINTURE

Map 6; 101 Rue Olivier des Serres, 15th; ///rudder.empires.data;
www.petiteceinture.org

Tucked away in the centre of Paris lies one of its best-kept secrets: an abandoned railway line, its disused tracks overgrown with wild flowers and its tunnels covered in graffiti. While it's slowly being redeveloped into walkable stretches, much of the Petite Ceinture still remains

Occupying the disused former Montrouge-Ceinture station along the Petite Ceinture is Poinçon Paris *(www.poincon paris.com)*, an oft-overlooked spot in the 14th. Colourful dining tables seat lunchers awaiting a "Jazz Brunch", while exhibitions and concerts draw in a trendy, vibrant crowd. If it's a sunny day, grab a table on the terrace by the train tracks.

off-limits – though an in-crowd of urban explorers know of the current access points in the 12th, 13th, 15th and 16th arrondissements. Decide which part to explore, then embark on a quiet hike (it can be quite rough at points). Should you need a refreshment, some of the old stations along the line in the north have been turned into cool bars.

SKATE WITH PARI ROLLER

Map 6; start at Place Raoul Dautry, 15th; ///turkeys.quiz.dusted;
www.pari-roller.com

Don't be alarmed when you see a rush of skaters flashing by in one protracted wave – it's just another Friday night with Pari Roller, Paris's premier skating event. It's free, so simply rent a pair of skates if you don't have your own and mingle with the hundreds of others laughing and chatting while the music blasts. What more exhilarating way is there to see all of Paris's major landmarks by moonlight?

HIKE THROUGH CIMETIÈRE DU PÈRE LACHAISE

Map 3; enter at Boulevard Ménilmontant, 20th; ///scouting.glad.souk

Cemeteries often instil dread in visitors, but this one is different, with mausoleums to Parisian politicians, artists and writers jutting out of the ground like mini temples. Hilly climbs, crumbling staircases and meandering paths make a walk here more athletic than you'd think; go off-road to get into the really interesting parts.

» Don't leave without looking for Jim Morrison's grave (it's a place of pilgrimage for rock fans, so it'll be the most crowded spot).

By the Water

*Paris grew from its river, and locals can hardly
resist the siren's call beckoning them to its edges.
Whether in it, on it or along it, you'll always find
a way to splash around the city's waterways.*

PISCINE MOLITOR

**Map 6; 13 Rue Nungesser et Coli, 16th; ///index.directly.petted;
www.mltr.fr**

You don't need to be a guest at the hotel attached to this open-air
pool to take a dip – much to the delight of well-heeled Parisians. The
place to be seen, this Art Deco haven attracts leisure-seekers who
sprawl across lounge chairs, sip on cocktails and get pampered in
the spa. It's a sophisticated (and splurge) alternative to the crowded
public pools, so maybe save it for when your mum or sister are in town.

PARC RIVES DE SEINE

Map 3; start at 2–4 Quai Henri IV, 4th; ///homework.scooter.years

Extending on both sides of the Seine, this riverside park is a favoured
local haunt whatever the season. During the summer, it's home to
Paris-Plages, a temporary artificial beach paradise that sees a
trendy crowd of students gossiping on deckchairs and large families

Have something to celebrate? Take a Seine champagne cruise with Ô Chateau for a bit of luxury while sightseeing.

picnicking under palm trees. The rest of the year you can expect a post-work crowd unwinding with a large glass of wine in the floating cafés and bars without the crush of crowds.

BASSIN DE L'ARSENAL

Map 3; enter at Place de la Bastille, 12th; ///focus.tablet.began

Linking the Canal Saint-Martin with the Seine, this little port is a popular hangout with a younger, edgier set of Parisians. Join them on a warm evening by grabbing a bottle of wine from nearby Les Caprices de l'Instant before claiming a spot on the cobblestones by the water. It won't be long before you're dreaming of having an apéritif on your own boat, like the many sailors you'll spot.

BASSIN DE LA VILLETTE

Map 5; enter at Quai de la Loire, 19th; ///bright.request.flesh

Lined with cafés, restaurants and two major cinemas, this artificial lake gives off a buzzing festival atmosphere year-round. Picnics and *pétanque* – a winning combination for Parisians – play out day and night on the banks, while the warmer weather also brings with it the northern outpost of the city's annual summer beach event, Paris-Plages. You can easily spend a day hanging around here if you want to play Parisian (just mind the cycle path, please).

» Don't leave without hiring an electric boat for a cruise, where you'll have access to 40 km (64 miles) of waterways.

Solo, Pair, Crowd

The beauty of Paris is the endless ways you can engage with the water, no matter what you're seeking.

SOLO
Night walk

Lean up against the railings of Pont Alexandre III, Paris's prettiest and most flamboyant Art Nouveau bridge, to see the city lights reflect in the water at night.

IN A PAIR
Row your boat

Splash along like a set of Pisces in a rowboat on the Lac Inférieur, the largest of the two lakes in the Bois de Boulogne *(p168)*. It's a favourite pastime for Parisians, especially on summer weekends.

FOR A CROWD
It's all fun and games

Les Berges de Seine on the Left Bank was made for families, with walls for climbing and games of hopscotch to keep the kids busy while parents sip on a coffee from one of the many cafés lining the banks.

PISCINE JOSÉPHINE BAKER

Map 6; Quai François Mauriac, 13th; ///stumpy.solar.spits;
www.piscine-baker.fr

This snazzy public pool actually floats in the Seine – kind of meta, right? It's open all year, but hots up in the summer when the roof rolls back and it's completely outdoors. It's a real community spot, where groups of friends go to cool off, those channelling their inner Joséphine Baker lounge on the sunbeds and kids splash about.

MARNE RIVER

Map 1; depart from Port Solferino, 7th; ///rested.touchy.neutron

Everyone heads to the Seine for boat tours of the big sights, but the Marne, which feeds into the Seine, is a provincial alternative for the nautically minded that few ever venture to navigate. Cruises head east, passing through greenery and locks, to the city's other river. It's a popular route for fans of Impressionism, who can seek the plays of light on the water that inspired the likes of Pissarro and Cézanne.

QUAI FRANÇOIS MAURIAC

Map 6; Quai François Mauriac, 13th; ///contents.search.arming

This riverfront promenade with barge cafés and summertime restaurants is decidedly local. It's the perfect place for a riverside stroll, whether you're catching up with a friend before crossing over to Parc de Bercy or taking your parents to dinner along the banks.

>> **Don't leave without** checking out its most famous occupant, the Batofar, which was the first serious nightclub housed on a boat.

Dreamy Viewpoints

Paris is (rightfully) known as one of the world's most beautiful cities, so it follows that a picturesque view is never hard to find. Everyone has their favourite pocket of the city to watch the sun set or gain perspective.

PARC DE SAINT-CLOUD

Map 6; enter at Avenue de la Grille d'Honneur, Saint-Cloud;
///junior.couple.grills; www.domaine-saint-cloud.fr

Those who live beyond the city limits proudly point out that this is the best place to see Paris in all its glory. Far enough from the inner city to provide sweeping panoramas, Parc de Saint-Cloud soars above the likes of the Eiffel Tower and Montmartre. After work, residents have one vantage point in mind: Rond Point de la Balustrade, to watch the sun set over the Seine.

THE STEPS OF THE SACRÉ-COEUR

Map 4; Parvis du Sacré-Coeur, 18th; ///products.minus.page

Forget climbing to the top of the dome for city views: the steps outside the basilica are where it's at. In the evening, groups of students, local workers and out-of-towners mingle on the steps here, while illicit but welcomed wine and beer sellers weave through them

Head here on New Year's Eve for a relaxed street party and great views of fireworks from across the city.

all selling drinks. It's a chilled spot to catch up while looking out over Paris's rooftops (including the big hitters, like the Notre Dame and Centre Pompidou).

SQUARE DU VERT-GALANT

Map 1; 15 Place du Pont Neuf, 1st; ///stoops.fake.shrimp

Hidden in plain sight at the end of Île de la Cité, this tiny park is one that many Parisians would rather keep to themselves, but it'd be foolish to withhold it. The narrow paths by the water that surround it are filled with revellers who couldn't nab a spot on the park's grassy stretch, but who aren't complaining either – they get the best views of the Louvre. The Parisian whimsy is in full throttle, with sunset ceding to the lights of passing boats as friends and couples soak it all in.

» Don't leave without picking up fresh supplies on your way here for a picnic, because watching the sunset is even better with cheese.

PASSERELLE RICHERAND

Map 5; Passerelle Richerand, Quai de Jemmapes, 10th;
///clubs.swam.coaster

Enticing both serious and budding photographers to rise early is a crowdless sunrise shot of the Canal Saint-Martin. What this footbridge lacks in beauty it makes up for in being the perfect point from which to capture the canal's other elegant bridges while the sun slowly rises above the water. Photos up here are especially striking under a rare covering of winter snow, especially if the water is frozen.

PARC DE BELLEVILLE

Map 5; 11 Rue Piat, 20th; ///racing.walled.beaters; 01 43 15 20 20

This park isn't the most beautiful – a blessing in disguise for avoiding crowds – but the views from the scruffy hilltop terrace are among the best in Paris. Rewarding the infrequent couples and friend sets who trek to the top of the steep hill are photograph-worthy views of Notre-Dame and the Eiffel Tower on the other side of the city.

» Don't leave without buying some cheap Vietnamese takeout from a restaurant in Belleville for good picnic sustenance while the sun sets.

LAMARCK–CAULAINCOURT

Map 4; Place Dalida, 18th; ///soup.cricket.bucks

Stretching north to the suburbs, the other side of the Butte Montmartre is the less-trodden (more thigh-screaming) alternative to the Sacré-Coeur steps. Proving that gorgeous views don't always equal city-wide panoramas, Lamarck-Caulaincourt is all about the scenic journey, where a walk down the steps passes café awnings framing the street as it drops away down the hill.

PONT DE BIR-HAKEIM

Map 6; Pont de Bir-Hakeim, 15th; ///paradise.wider.shape

While out-of-towners scale the Eiffel Tower's full height, locals come to this bridge to see it from a distance – it's the most unobstructed view of the iconic structure you'll find. Nothing says Paris quite like being perched under hanging street lights and looking out over the Iron Lady at night, the occasional metro rattling overhead.

Liked by the locals

"I stop by Parc de Belleville most days, often timing my walk home so I can lean on the railings and watch the Eiffel Tower sparkle at night. There's nowhere better to get a feel for the *quartier*."

ELEANOR JOY, WRITER AND BELLEVILLE RESIDENT

Streets and Squares

Tangles of cobbled roads in hidden districts spill into leafy squares and passages in Paris. These are the threads that hold together the fabric of the city, a geography designed for a flâneur *(aimless wanderer).*

BUTTE-AUX-CAILLES

Map 6; 2 Rue de la Butte aux Cailles, 13th; ///trumped.global.swerves

This lesser-known neighbourhood, happily often overlooked by visitors, is loved by locals for its tight-knit community feel. Strolling through feels like wandering a quiet country town, but with an unexpected artistic edge: quirky restaurants line narrow cobbleston lanes, street art fills nearly every corner and laidback bars attract students hoping to bask in the sun. It's all very chill, almost hippy.

GALERIE VIVIENNE

Map 1; 5 Rue de la Banque, 2nd; ///folders.emperor.slices; www.galerie-vivienne.com

The Neo-Classical shopping arcades built in the 19th century were once the stuff of high society, combining the Parisian pastimes of a *flânerie* and sophisticated shopping trips. These "passages" are few and far between today (no thanks to department stores), but this chic arcade – the best-preserved in Paris – is a firm favourite for those seeking a bit of sophistication and an escape from modern life. An amble on the mosaic floors, a dip into Librairie Jousseaume *(p97)* and a refreshing glass of wine truly transport you to a bygone era.

RUE MONTORGUEIL

Map 1; start at Quartier Montorgueil, 2nd; ///pricing.rates.mass
A buzzing village-like nook in the centre of Paris, this café-lined road has always been a stronghold of community spirit and life. Once a main artery into the former Les Halles market, it remains a food-focused district today, with shops dedicated to French classics drawing both young and old residents. It's the people you meet that shape a visit here, whether it's cheese shop owners with tempting tasting trays in the day or post-work revellers laughing from the restaurant terraces come evening.

» Don't leave without picking up a heavenly pastry from Stoeher, the oldest bakery in Paris, to accompany you on your stroll.

RUE DES BARRES

Map 2; start N, off Rue François Miron, 4th; ///peachy.crunch.stealing
One of the oldest streets in central Paris, Rue des Barres gives off major history book vibes. A wander through this short passageway is like walking along a timeline: you'll pass half-timbered houses that date back to the 1500s, peek at a church that survived a stray shell from World War I and end up at the Parc Rives de Seine *(p172)*, where modern life plays out at its best.

LA CAMPAGNE À PARIS

Map 6; enter at the stairs, 2–4 Rue Geo Chavez, 20th;
///yell.hurray.drones

It's fitting that the name of this outer district, tucked away in the 20th, translates to "the countryside in Paris". Time seems to stand still in this haven of peace, where you won't find any shops or monuments, simply flower-adorned houses where Parisians live their lives in tranquillity. Few travellers venture this far east, so you'll have it all to yourself (or at least shared with a few locals who, you know, live here).

PASSAGE BRADY

Map 5; 46 Rue du Faubourg Saint-Denis, 10th; ///shared.victory.glosses

The sweet smell of onions gently browning with fragrant spices is the first sign that you're in the *quartier* often dubbed "Little India". Passage Brady has long been at the heart of the Indian community in Paris – and is loved by locals partial to a good biryani. Unlike other passages prettified for visitors, this one is unpretentious, where 100 types of incense and the sounds of Indian music accompany a stroll through.

RUE DES MARTYRS

Map 4; start S, off Rue Lamartine, 9th; ///bills.reward.gestures

A hot contender for Paris's loveliest street (heck, there's even been a whole book written about it), this sloping lane has become more popular than Parisians would like in recent years. Despite growing gentrification, though, it manages to hold onto its old-school charm. Dedicated residents are to thank for that, who dart between the time-honoured stores along this road every morning, picking up flowers, daily baguettes and the odd roasted chicken from familiar faces. Leisurely ambling through offers a true snapshot of local life.

» Don't leave without walking to the top of the street to Montmartre's famed *je t'aime* wall, where "I love you" is painted in over 300 languages. Sure, it's been photographed countless times, but it's cute.

PLACE DAUPHINE

Map 1; enter by Rue Henri-Robert, Île de la Cité, 1st; ///referral.careful.stews

Towered over by tall buildings, galleries and restaurants, this triangular-shaped square is secluded enough to feel worlds away from the bustle of the 1st. It might be tiny, but it packs a punch: old boys play *pétanque* on the sandy plaza, dog walkers take to the cobblestone streets surrounding it and lawyers working at the nearby Palace of Justice relax under café awnings. You could circle it five times and never tire of the ambience — it's authentic Paris at its best.

Though many Parisians know of Hôtel Dieu, the city's oldest hospital, many unknowingly stroll past the inner courtyard that lies just past the entry. Walking through the square feels akin to being in the grounds of an impressive palace, with manicured shrubs surrounding the hospital's Romanesque arches. If hospitals don't give you the creeps, visit this square at lunchtime for a leisurely saunter and a slice of calm.

Nearby Getaways

*Parisians are incredibly fond of their city, but they're
just as much in love with their country. With so many
options for day trips from the centre, they're never
short of somewhere to go for that breath of fresh air.*

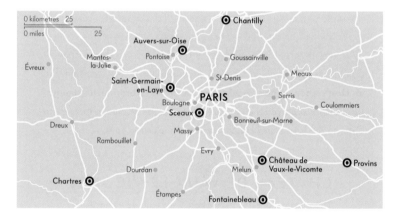

CHANTILLY

20 minutes from Gare du Nord station; www.chantilly-tourisme.com

Paris may have won the moniker for the most romantic city, but the
couples who flock here on weekend trips would argue otherwise.
A classy combination of château, park and forest, the very fabric of
this village was made for romance. Early risers watch the sun come

up over the garden's calm lake, foodies tuck into strawberries with the estate's namesake *crème chantilly*, and country guys and girls at heart stroll the stables – this is the horse-racing capital of France, after all – to catch one of the dressage demonstrations.

AUVERS-SUR-OISE

1 hour from Gare du Nord station

It's hard to tire of Paris's art scene, but when the thought of a stuffy, crowded gallery fills you with dread, this picturesque village – a favourite of the Impressionists – is the perfect antidote. As you stroll the cutesy, quaint streets and the manicured gardens of the Château d'Auvers, it's easy to see why Cézanne and Pissarro were inspired to paint here – and why Van Gogh described it as "seriously beautiful".

» Don't leave without visiting the Musée de l'Absinthe. It's thought that this spirit played a large role in Van Gogh's suicide in Auvers-sur-Oise, so the town's arty connection continues even here.

CHÂTEAU DE VAUX-LE-VICOMTE

1 hour from Gare de l'Est station; www.vaux-le-vicomte.com

Let the out-of-towners take over Versailles; this seriously underrated rural château is a local secret. It's a winner throughout the seasons: in the spring, kids excitedly tackle the Easter egg hunt; in the summer, groups of girlfriends sip champagne on candlelit evenings; come winter, it's a playground for all to get into the holiday spirit. Inside, fires crackle, carols play and nutmeg wafts through the air, and as dusk falls, the trees outside light up in what becomes a magical wonderland.

CHARTRES

1.5 hours from Gare du Nord station

Picture a classic, quaint medieval town and you've got Chartres: a towering Gothic cathedral, cobblestone streets lined with half-timbered houses and footbridges spanning the pretty waterside. This is the tranquil day trip Parisians embark on after a long work week, getting swept up in the calm of it all and letting their feet (and mind) wander. Hey, the *flâneur* isn't only found in Paris.

» Don't leave without picking up a Chartres speciality, *le cochelin* – a human-shaped flaky pastry filled with jam.

SCEAUX

30 minutes from Gare du Nord station

When city slickers are seeking a dose of nature outside Paris, Sceaux is their first port of call. The Parc de Sceaux, an under-the-radar estate housing a tiny château and formal gardens, comes alive at the weekend when bird-watchers, strollers and cyclists take over the grassy expanses. During the spring, you may struggle to find space on the lawns, given the amount of gourmet picnics that are set up underneath the cherry blossom trees.

PROVINS

1.5 hours from Gare de l'Est station; www.provins.net

This former Roman outpost offers much more than its famous ramparts and towers. Sure, there's plenty of architecture to admire, but the tours of the vaulted underground passages beneath the city

Visit on a Wednesday or Saturday for the market, where you can pick up fresh cheese and seafood.

are where it's at. Dark, spooky and chilly (even in the summer), these tunnels were once warehouses where merchants would store their goods. Bring a jumper.

FONTAINEBLEAU

40 minutes from Gare de Lyon station; www.fontainebleau.fr

Escaping the city hubbub has always been the main reason to visit this ancient royal city: once for the upper classes, now for all walks of life. The château here undoubtedly hogs the headlines, given its 1,500 rooms, all styled over the centuries by various French monarchs. But most Parisians skip it altogether, rather donning their walking boots and heading to the forest that surrounds it – it's the largest natural area of the Île-de-France region. You're likely to pass climbers as you amble through the sun-dappled forest floor, home as it is to tens of thousands of boulders. If you're seeking a thrill, why not give it a go?

SAINT-GERMAIN-EN-LAYE

30 minutes from Gare de Lyon station

History-loving parents coming to town? This charming little suburb is worth a trip. First off, there's the château. Not only is this where Louis XIV was born, it's now home to France's national archaeological museum, where artifacts go back to the Palaeolithic times. Then there's the Maison Debussy, where composer Claude Debussy was born (yep, another name drop) and his manuscripts and personal possessions still call home. How's that for history?

Scale:
0 metres 400
0 yards 400

BLVD SÉRURIER

19TH

**Fantasize through
LA MOUZAÏA**

Finish up with a meander
through this small bucolic
district of cobbled lanes,
picking out your dream
home and pretty garden.

5

RUE DU GÉNÉRAL BRUNET

RUE MANIN

RUE DE CRIMÉE

**Midday snack at
PARC DES BUTTES-
CHAUMONT**

Tuck into food with a
backdrop of greenery at
Pavillon Puebla, then
walk it off around the
park's romantic lake.

4

RUE BOTZARIS

RUE FESSART

PLACE DES
FÊTES

*Renowned French
singer-songwriter Edith
Piaf was born at **72 Rue
de Belleville**, marked
now by a plaque
above the door.*

BELLEVILLE

RUE DE BELLEVILLE

3

**Mooch around
JOURDAIN**

Stroll through this village-like
sub-neighbourhood, window-
shopping in the artists' ateliers
hidden on Rue de la Villette.

20TH

RUE PIAT

**Enjoy the view from
PARC DE BELLEVILLE**

After climbing to the top of this
steep park, settle on the grass
and look out to the Eiffel Tower.

2

RUE DES COURONNES

*Lamp-lined alleys
like **Passage Plantin**
have changed little
since Belleville was
outside the city limits,
before 1860.*

**Amble along the
PETITE CEINTURE**

Go in search of the few walkable
sections of the railway that once
encircled Paris. It's slowly being
reclaimed and is covered in graffiti.

1

11TH

RUE OBERKAMPF

MÉNILMONTANT

A morning flânerie through
edgy Belleville

Belleville, as Parisians from other neighbourhoods tend to say, is a *quartier qui bouge:* a lively part of town, as busy at 2am as it is at 10am. It spans two of the most diverse arrondissements, the 19th and 20th, where in the space of a few streets you find yourself walking down forgotten cobblestone lanes, past rows of Chinese supermarkets and alongside locals sporting trendy "looks" that wouldn't be out of place in London's Shoreditch or NYC's Brooklyn. There's nowhere better to see the real Paris and let yourself get lost for the day.

1. La Petite Ceinture
60 Rue de
Ménilmontant, 20th
///terminology.careful.pens

2. Parc de Belleville
11 Rue Piat, 20th
///racing.walled.beaters

3. Jourdain
Rue du Jourdain, 20th
///private.messing.stud

4. Parc des Buttes-Chaumont
1 Rue Botzaris, 19th
///contour.regime.liners

5. La Mouzaïa
///rapid.nail.paraded

72 Rue de Belleville
///took.human.rattler

With a little research and preparation, this city will feel like a home away from home. Check out these websites to ensure a healthy, safe stay in Paris.

Paris
DIRECTORY

SAFE SPACES

Paris is generally a welcoming city, but should you feel uneasy at any point or want to find your community, there are spaces catering to different genders, sexualities, demographics and religions.

www.centrelgbtparis.org
Centre running events and offering support for the LGBT+ community.

www.cjl-paris.org
Jewish community centre led by the first female rabbi of France.

www.espacesantetrans.fr
Project to improve healthcare for trans people in France, with a helpline.

www.icsparis.com
A non-profit offering mental health support for English speakers.

www.inter-lgbt.org
Organizers of the annual Paris Pride.

HEALTH

Healthcare in France is pricey, so take out comprehensive health insurance; EU residents can register for a European Health Insurance Card (EHIC) and UK citizens can apply for the UK Global Health Insurance Card (GHIC) to get discounted or free care. If you do need medical assistance, there are many pharmacies and hospitals across town.

www.3237.fr
Pharmacies open outside normal hours.

www.ameli.fr
Official portal for healthcare in France.

www.american-hospital.org
Paris's largest English-speaking hospital.

www.doctolib.fr
Book appointments with local clinics, including dentists and doctors.

www.pourvous.croix-rouge.fr
Red Cross, an English-friendly clinic with sexual health testing and advice.

www.sosmedecins.fr/en
24/7 home visits for situations not requiring an ambulance; call-out fees from €80.

TRAVEL SAFETY ADVICE
Before you travel – and while you're here – always keep tabs on France's latest regulations.

www.diplomatie.gouv.fr
Information from the French government on travel to, and living in, France.

www.gov.uk/foreign-travel-advice
Up-to-date travel advice from the FCO.

www.gouvernement.fr
The French government website, the first port of call for COVID-19 regulations.

www.prefecturedepolice. interieur.gouv.fr
The Préfecture's tips for staying safe and what to do if you're a victim of crime.

www.solidaritefemmes.org
Resources and a helpline for female victims of violence.

ACCESSIBILITY
Provision for those with reduced mobility remains very poor in Paris, particularly on public transport. The below websites provide useful resources to make exploring the city easier.

www.g7.fr
Company offering accessible taxis for those with specific requirements.

www.handicap.monuments-nationaux.fr
French-only information for people with specific requirements when visiting sites.

www.jaccede.com/en
Crowd-sourced details of accessible museums, bars, restaurants and cinemas.

www.parisinfo.com
Official resource for visiting Paris, with an annually updated downloadable guide for travelling with specific requirements.

www.ratp.fr
Information on public transport options for those with reduced mobility or impaired sight.

ABOUT THE ILLUSTRATOR

Mantas Tumosa

Creative designer and illustrator Mantas moved from his home country of Lithuania to London back in 2011. By day, he's busy creating bold, minimalistic illustrations that tell a story – such as the gorgeous cover of this book. By night, he's dreaming of adventures away, catching up on the basketball and cooking Italian food (which he can't get enough of).

Main Contributors Yuki Higashinakano, Bryan Pirolli

Senior Editor Lucy Richards

Senior Designer Tania Gomes

Project Editor Zoë Rutland

Project Art Editor Bharti Karakoti

Editor Lucy Sara-Kelly

Proofreader Stephanie Smith

Senior Cartographic Editor Casper Morris

Cartography Manager Suresh Kumar

Cartographer Ashif

Jacket Designer Tania Gomes

Jacket Illustrator Mantas Tumosa

Senior Production Editor Jason Little

Senior Production Controller Stephanie McConnell

Managing Editor Hollie Teague

Managing Art Editor Bess Daly

Art Director Maxine Pedliham

Publishing Director Georgina Dee

First edition 2021

Published in Great Britain by Dorling Kindersley Limited,
DK, One Embassy Gardens, 8 Viaduct Gardens,
London SW11 7BW.

The authorised representative in the EEA is
Dorling Kindersley Verlag GmbH. Arnulfstr. 124,
80636 Munich, Germany.

Published in the United States by DK Publishing,
1450 Broadway, Suite 801, New York, NY 10018.

Copyright © 2021 Dorling Kindersley Limited
A Penguin Random House Company
21 22 23 24 10 9 8 7 6 5 4 3 2

The publishers cannot accept responsibility for any consequences arising from
the use of this book, nor for any material on third party websites, and cannot
guarantee that any website address in this book will be a suitable source of
travel information.

A CIP catalog record for this book is available from the British Library.

A catalog record for this book is available from the Library of Congress.

ISSN: 1542 1554
ISBN: 978 0 2414 9069 3

Printed and bound in Canada.

www.dk.com

A NOTE FROM DK EYEWITNESS

The world is fast-changing and it's keeping us folk at
DK Eyewitness on our toes. We've worked hard to ensure
that this edition of Paris Like a Local is up-to-date and
reflects today's favourite places but we know that standards
shift, venues close and new ones pop up in their place. So, if
you notice something has closed, we've got something
wrong or left something out, we want to hear about it.
Please drop us a line at travelguides@dk.com